First World War
and Army of Occupation
War Diary
France, Belgium and Germany

28 DIVISION
84 Infantry Brigade
Cheshire Regiment
2nd Battalion
2 February 1915 - 31 October 1915

WO95/2276/2

The Naval & Military Press Ltd
www.nmarchive.com
Published in association with The National Archives

Published by

The Naval & Military Press Ltd

Unit 10 Ridgewood Industrial Park,

Uckfield, East Sussex,

TN22 5QE England

Tel: +44 (0) 1825 749494

www.naval-military-press.com

www.nmarchive.com

This diary has been reprinted in facsimile from the original. Any imperfections are inevitably reproduced and the quality may fall short of modern type and cartographic standards.

© **Crown Copyright**
Images reproduced by permission of The National Archives, London, England, 2015.

Contents

Document type	Place/Title	Date From	Date To
Heading	95/2276 2/Cheshires Feb 15-Oct 15		
Heading	28th Division 84th Infy Bde 2nd Bn Cheshire Regt Feb-Oct 1915		
Heading	28th Div. 84th Bde. Note: 84th Bde Came under Order of 5th Division. 22.2.15.		
War Diary	Merris	02/02/1915	02/02/1915
War Diary	Ham	03/02/1915	03/02/1915
War Diary	Night	04/02/1915	12/02/1915
War Diary	Ouderdom	14/02/1915	15/02/1915
War Diary	Krusstadt.	16/02/1915	27/02/1915
Heading	5th Div. 928 84th Bde. War Diary 2nd Cheshire Regt. March 1915 Attached. Operation Orders.		
War Diary		01/03/1915	07/03/1915
War Diary	Bailleul	08/03/1915	14/03/1915
War Diary	Petit Pont	14/03/1915	14/03/1915
War Diary	Romarin	15/03/1915	15/03/1915
War Diary	Ploegsteert.	16/03/1915	17/03/1915
War Diary	Bailleul	18/03/1915	19/03/1915
War Diary	Kemmel	19/03/1915	24/03/1915
War Diary	Dranoutre	25/03/1915	28/03/1915
War Diary	Lindenhoek	28/03/1915	31/03/1915
Heading	Operation Orders.		
Miscellaneous	2 Ches R. O.O. No 15.	19/03/1915	19/03/1915
Miscellaneous	2 Ches R. O.O. No 15	21/03/1915	21/03/1915
Miscellaneous	2 Ches Regt O.O. No 17	22/03/1915	22/03/1915
Miscellaneous	2nd Ches R. O.O. No. 18	23/03/1915	23/03/1915
Operation(al) Order(s)	Cheshire Regt. Operation Order No. 19	24/03/1915	24/03/1915
Miscellaneous	R. O.O. 21	29/03/1915	29/03/1915
Miscellaneous	R.O.O. 22	30/03/1915	30/03/1915
Miscellaneous	Regt O.O. No. 22	30/03/1915	30/03/1915
Heading	28th Div. 84th Bde. Note. 84th Bde rejoined 28th Div from 5th Div. on 6th April		
War Diary	Lindenhoek	01/04/1915	01/04/1915
War Diary	Branoutee	02/04/1915	03/04/1915
War Diary	Bailleul.	06/04/1915	12/04/1915
War Diary	Vlamertinghe	12/04/1915	15/04/1915
War Diary	Zonebeke	16/04/1915	16/04/1915
War Diary	Molenaarelsthoek	16/04/1915	17/04/1915
War Diary	St. Jean	18/04/1915	22/04/1915
War Diary	Frezenberg	23/04/1915	23/04/1915
War Diary	Zonnebeke	23/04/1915	30/04/1915
Heading	28th Div. 84th Bde. War Diary 2nd Cheshire Regt. May 1915		
War Diary	Zonnebeke	26/04/1915	04/05/1915
War Diary	Potijze	05/05/1915	07/05/1915
War Diary	Verlorenhoek	07/05/1915	10/05/1915
War Diary	Ypres	10/05/1915	11/05/1915
War Diary	Poperinghe	12/05/1915	12/05/1915
War Diary	Boenhaert	13/05/1915	13/05/1915
War Diary	Brandhoek.	15/05/1915	19/05/1915

War Diary	Herzeele	20/05/1915	23/05/1915
War Diary	Brandhoek	23/05/1915	23/05/1915
War Diary	Ypres	25/05/1915	25/05/1915
War Diary	Brandhoek	25/05/1915	28/05/1915
War Diary	Herzeele	29/05/1915	31/05/1915
Heading	28th Div. 84th Bde. War Diary. 2nd Cheshire Regt. June 1915		
War Diary	Herzeele	30/05/1915	11/06/1915
War Diary	Reninghelst.	12/06/1915	12/06/1915
War Diary	Voormezeele	13/06/1915	13/06/1915
War Diary	Dickebusch	13/06/1915	30/06/1915
Heading	28th Div. 84th Bde. War Diary. 2nd Cheshire Regt. July. 1915 Attached. Operation Orders.		
War Diary	Dickebusch	30/06/1915	13/07/1915
War Diary	Rosendael Beek	14/07/1915	14/07/1915
War Diary	Westoutre	15/07/1915	15/07/1915
War Diary	Kemmel	16/07/1915	20/07/1915
War Diary	Locre	21/07/1915	27/07/1915
War Diary	Trenches	28/07/1915	31/07/1915
Heading	Operation Orders.		
Operation(al) Order(s)	Operation Order No. 45 Copy No. 1 by Major Goodwyn. Commd 2 Cheshire	27/07/1914	27/07/1914
Operation(al) Order(s)	Operation Order No. 39 by Brigadier-General L.J. Bols, C.B., D.S.O., Commanding 84th Infantry Brigade.	27/07/1915	27/07/1915
Miscellaneous	Table "A" Garrison.		
Heading	28th Div. 84th Bde. War Diary. 2nd Cheshire Regt. August 1915. Attached Operation Orders.		
War Diary	Trenches Near Kemmel	01/08/1915	04/08/1915
War Diary	Locre	06/08/1915	07/08/1915
War Diary	Kemmel Shelters	07/08/1915	09/08/1915
War Diary	Kemmel	11/08/1915	11/08/1915
War Diary	Kemmel Shelters.	11/08/1915	11/08/1915
War Diary	Trenches Near Lindenhoek.	12/08/1915	17/08/1915
War Diary	Locre	19/08/1915	31/08/1915
Heading	Operation Orders.		
Operation(al) Order(s)	Operation Order No. 40	02/08/1915	02/08/1915
Miscellaneous	Garrison.		
Operation(al) Order(s)	Operation Order No. 41 by Brigadier-General L.J. Bols, C.B., D.S.O. Commanding 84th Infantry Brigade.	08/08/1915	08/08/1915
Miscellaneous	28th Division. Training of 37th Division in trench warfare.		
Operation(al) Order(s)	Operation Order No. 42 by Brigadier-General L.J. Bols, C.B., D.S.O., Commanding 84th Infantry Brigade.	10/08/1915	10/08/1915
Miscellaneous			
Operation(al) Order(s)	Operation Order No. 43 by Brigadier-General L.J. Bols, C.B., D.S.O., Commanding 84th Infantry Brigade.	14/08/1915	14/08/1915
Operation(al) Order(s)	Operation Order No. 44 by Brigadier-General L.J. Bols C.B., D.S.O., Commanding 84th Infantry Brigade.	17/08/1915	17/08/1915
Operation(al) Order(s)	Operation Order No. 46 by Brigadier-General L.J. Bols, C.B., D.S.O., Commanding 84th Infantry Brigade.	21/08/1915	21/08/1915
Operation(al) Order(s)	Operation Order No. 47 by Brigadier-General L.J. Bols, C.B., D.S.O., Commanding 84th Infantry Brigade.	23/08/1915	23/08/1915
Operation(al) Order(s)	Operation Order No. 49 by Lieut. Colonel T.H. Finch-Pearse, C.M.G., Commanding 84th Infantry Brigade.	28/08/1915	28/08/1915
Operation(al) Order(s)	Operation Order No. 11 by Major Goodwin Commdg.	03/08/1915	03/08/1915

Operation(al) Order(s)	Operation Order No 10 by Lieut T.H.F Pearse C.M.G. Commdg, L.B., Cheshire Regt	11/08/1915	11/08/1915
Miscellaneous	Schedule of Trenches No. 1 Group.		
Miscellaneous	Operation Order No. 11	13/08/1915	13/08/1915
Miscellaneous	From To Reliefing After Relief		
Operation(al) Order(s)	2nd Cheshire Regiment Operation Order No. 13	18/08/1915	18/08/1915
Miscellaneous	Grenades Nomenclature of (G.R.O.899) the		
Operation(al) Order(s)	2nd Bn. Cheshire Regiment Operation Orders	24/08/1915	24/08/1915
Miscellaneous	The Officer Comdg 1st Bn Suffolk. Regt.	25/08/1915	25/08/1915
Operation(al) Order(s)	2nd Cheshire Regiment Operation Order No 14	29/08/1915	29/08/1915
Map	Sheet II		
Operation(al) Order(s)	Operation Order No 20 by:- Lieut St. M.G. White D.S.O. Commanding Suffolk Regiment.	29/08/1915	29/08/1915
Miscellaneous	2 Ches O.O. No. 14 Ref Map 28	31/08/1915	31/08/1915
Heading	84th Bde. 28th Div. 2nd Cheshires September 1915		
Heading	On His Majesty's Service.		
War Diary	Kemmel Shelters	01/09/1915	02/09/1915
War Diary	Trenches Near Lindenhoek.	03/09/1915	07/09/1915
War Diary	Locre.	09/09/1915	14/09/1915
War Diary	Trenches Near Lindenhoek.	15/09/1915	20/09/1915
War Diary	Locre.	21/09/1915	21/09/1915
War Diary	Borre.	23/09/1915	27/09/1915
War Diary	Sailly-La-Bourse.	27/09/1915	29/09/1915
War Diary	Annequin	30/09/1915	30/09/1915
Miscellaneous	2 Ches R. O.O. No 15	01/09/1915	01/09/1915
Miscellaneous	Trench Sheet this		
Miscellaneous	Amended Schedule		
Miscellaneous	2 Ches R. O.O. No 16	09/09/1915	09/09/1915
Miscellaneous	2 Ches R. O.O. No 17	12/09/1915	12/09/1915
Operation(al) Order(s)	2nd Battalion Cheshire Regt Operation Order No 18	13/09/1915	13/09/1915
Miscellaneous	Trench Strength Minimum Garrisons		
Operation(al) Order(s)	2nd Cheshire Rgt. Operation Order	19/09/1915	19/09/1915
Operation(al) Order(s)	Cheshire Regt	26/09/1915	26/09/1915
Operation(al) Order(s)	Operation Order No. 59 by Brigadier-General T.H. Finch-Pearse, C.M.G., Commanding 84th Infantry Brigade.	20/09/1915	20/09/1915
Operation(al) Order(s)	Operation Order No. 50 by Lieutenant-Colonel T.H. Finch-Pearse, C.M.G., Commanding 84th Infantry Brigade.	01/09/1915	01/09/1915
Operation(al) Order(s)	Operation Order No. 51 by Lieutenant-Colonel T.H. Finch-Pearse, C.M.G, Commanding 84th Infantry Brigade.	02/09/1915	02/09/1915
Miscellaneous	Trench. Garrison Remarks. Held by.		
Operation(al) Order(s)	Operation Order No. 52 by Brigadier-General L.J. Bols, C.B., D.S.O., Commanding 84th Infantry Brigade.	04/09/1915	04/09/1915
Operation(al) Order(s)	Operation Order No. 53 by Brigadier-General L.J. Bols, C.B., D.S.O., Commanding 84th Infantry Brigade.	07/09/1915	07/09/1915
Operation(al) Order(s)	Operation Order No. 54 by Lieut. Colonel T.H. Finch-Pearse, C.M.G., Commanding 84th Infantry Brigade.	10/09/1915	10/09/1915
Operation(al) Order(s)	Operation Order No. 55 by Lieutenant-Colonel T.H. Finch Pearse, C.M.G., Commanding 84th Infantry Brigade.	11/09/1915	11/09/1915
Operation(al) Order(s)	Operation Order No. 56 by Lieutenant-Colonel T.H. Finch-Pearse, C.M.G., Commanding 84th Infantry Brigade.	13/09/1915	13/09/1915

Operation(al) Order(s)	Operation Order No 57. by Lieut-Colonel Finch-Pearse, C.M.G., Commanding 84th Infantry Brigade.	16/09/1915	16/09/1915
Heading	Major Hill Diary		
Miscellaneous	To. 2nd Coles Inf. Regt.	18/09/1915	18/09/1915
Miscellaneous	Guide. Trench. Guides for trench. Guides for M.G.		
Operation(al) Order(s)	Operation Order No. 58 by Brigadier-General T.H. Finch-Pearse, C.M.G. Commanding 84th Infantry Brigade.	19/09/1915	19/09/1915
Miscellaneous	C.L. 286		
Miscellaneous	Reliefs, etc.	19/09/1915	19/09/1915
Operation(al) Order(s)	Operation Order No. 60. by Brigadier-General T.H. Finch-Pearse, C.M.G., Commanding 84th Infantry Brigade.	26/09/1915	26/09/1915
Operation(al) Order(s)	84th Infantry Brigade Operation Order No. 62	29/09/1915	29/09/1915
Operation(al) Order(s)	84th Bde. Operation Order No. 67	05/10/1915	05/10/1915
Miscellaneous		01/10/1915	01/10/1915
Heading	84th Bde. 28th Div. Embarked with Bde. for Salonika 24.10.15. 2nd Cheshires October 1915		
War Diary	Trenches Hohenzollern Redoubt	01/10/1915	08/10/1915
War Diary	Busnes	09/10/1915	18/10/1915
War Diary	Hinges	19/10/1915	19/10/1915
War Diary	LeQuesnoy	20/10/1915	21/10/1915
War Diary	On Train	22/10/1915	23/10/1915
War Diary	Marseilles	24/10/1915	24/10/1915
War Diary	S.S. Ivernia	24/10/1915	30/10/1915
War Diary	Marmoura Camp	31/10/1915	31/10/1915

95/2276
2/Cheshires
Feb '15 - Oct '15

28TH DIVISION
84TH INFY BDE

2ND BN CHESHIRE REGT
FEB - OCT 1915

TO SALONIKA

28th Div.
84th Bde.

Note:- 84th Bde came under Order of 5th Division. 22.2.15.

WAR DIARY.

2nd CHESHIRE REGT.

FEBRUARY.
1915.

Army Form C. 2118.

WAR DIARY
or
INTELLIGENCE SUMMARY.
(Erase heading not required.)

Instructions regarding War Diaries and Intelligence Summaries are contained in F. S. Regs., Part II, and the Staff Manual respectively. Title pages will be prepared in manuscript.

Hour, Date, Place.	Summary of Events and Information.	Remarks and references to Appendices.
MERRIS 11 AM 2nd Feb.	The Battn. left MERRIS and a forward up in Brigade at ROUGE CROIX from which place it proceeded by motor bus to being to YPRES. Officers with Bn. Major [STONE] (Commanding) Capt. HUGHES - TURNER HILL (Adjutant) MORTON - SAVAGE MAXIMON (Transport Officer) MAXWELL (2nd Lieut) WILL (Machine Gun Officer) MASON. VILLIERS-STUART ANDREWS - NEVINGTON - WATSON. CLARKE. LAW - 2 Lieuts KEATING WARD. G. KEATING - Lt (?) qm CONAN. Capt [McEWEN] RAMC. The transport under Capt. MALLINSON left the previous evening	Appx
6 P.M. 2 Feb.	Arrived at VLAMERTINGHE [where tea, rations + ammunition was issued]	
8 P.M. 2 Feb.	marched to YPRES.	
11 P.M. 2 Feb.	Left YPRES & march to take over trenches from French. Head quarters established VERBODEN MOLEN.	R.H.
4 AM 3 Feb.	Relief of trenches completed	R.A
Night 4-5 Feb.	The Battn. on relief of Suffolk Regt. proceeds (less 2 Coys) to YPRES as Reserve. 2 Companies (3+4) under Major STONE to BLAUWEPORT as support.	R.A
Night 5-6 Feb.	two 3+4 companies ordered up to support SUFFOLK Regt.	R.H.

Army Form C. 2118.

WAR DIARY
or
INTELLIGENCE SUMMARY.

(Erase heading not required.)

Instructions regarding War Diaries and Intelligence Summaries are contained in F. S. Regs., Part II, and the Staff Manual respectively. Title pages will be prepared in manuscript.

Hour, Date, Place.	Summary of Events and Information.	Remarks and references to Appendices.
Night 6-7 Feb.	The Bn relieved SUFFOLK Reg. in the trenches taking up the same disposition as before.	R.A.
Night 8-9 Feb.	The Bn less 2 companies moved to YPRES as reserve. 2 Companies (under Capt HUGHES) to BLAUWEPORT as support.	R.A.
Night 10-11 Feb.	The Bn relieved SUFFOLK Reg. in the trenches taking up the same disposition as before.	R.A.
Night 11-12 Feb. OUDERDOM	The Bn relieved by K.O.Y.L.I. (83rd Bde) marched to billets round OUDERDOM via YPRES	R.A.
1 p.m 14 Feb	Orders received to be ready to move at ½ hour notice as reports had been received that 23rd Bde had evacuated a trench.	R.A. 9/9/15
3.30 AM 15 Feb	Battalion ordered to move at once to YPRES	R.A.
5.30 AM 15 Feby.	Battalion moved off to YPRES [and on arrival proceeded to Infantry Barracks]	R.A.
	Subsequently the Battalion moved into billets at KRUISSTRAAT in support of 1st Suffolk Reg.	R.A.

1

Army Form C. 2118.

WAR DIARY
or
INTELLIGENCE SUMMARY.
(Erase heading not required.)

Instructions regarding War Diaries and Intelligence Summaries are contained in F. S. Regs., Part II, and the Staff Manual respectively. Title pages will be prepared in manuscript.

Hour, Date, Place.	Summary of Events and Information.	Remarks and references to Appendices.
KRUSSTADT.		
16th Feb.	The Battalion was ordered to relieve 1st Suffolk Regt. in the trenches. This order was subsequently cancelled, instructions were received to relieve Welch Regt. on left sector instead.	
5.30 p.m. 16 Feb.	The Battn. left KRUSSTADT & marched to Supp. Bks YPRES where 2 days rations ammn & water etc were drawn.	2/Lt
8 p.m. 16 Feb.	The above orders were cancelled & the following substituted. Two Companies (Nos 2 & 3) to march to H.Q. 9th Suffolk R. The combination with 1 Coy Suffolk Regt to take a German trench. One Coy. (No 1) to march to LANGEMARK Farm in support. One Coy. (No 4) to draw rations for 3 Coys Suffolks & 1 Coy Mercer R. & convey same to dug outs Sq I 33 & 3.3 (Belgian map 28) at which point the Coy remained in support. The attack of Nos 2 & 3 Companies was checked by hostile machine guns which opened at short range. Amongst the casualties were 2/Lt G. KEATING & 2/Lt J. KEATING killed & 2/Lt WARD wounded.	2/Lt

WAR DIARY or INTELLIGENCE SUMMARY.

Army Form C. 2118.

(Erase heading not required.)

Hour, Date, Place.	Summary of Events and Information.	Remarks and references to Appendices.
1915 7.30 A.M. 17 Feb	The Batt. assembled at CHATEAU ROSENTHAL in support of Welsh Reg.	
9 p.m. 17 Feb	The Bn less 1 Company (No 4) moved out to relieve the Welsh R in the trenches on N. side of canal - No 4 Coy was detached to a trench on S. side of canal.	R.M.
2.0 Feb.	Relieved from trenches by Welsh Reg.	
4 p.m. 20 Feb	Called out to support Welsh Reg.	R.M.
12.30 P.M. 21 Feb	No 1 Coy had 1 platoon in trench acct 1 in support. No 2 Company seeming to attack a trench evacuated by Welsh Reg. No 3 & 4 Coy remain in support of No 2 Coy. No 2 Coy occupied trench without loss & No 3 & 4 remained in support until daylight when a small force was left in	R.M.
7.30 a.m. 21 Feb.	The firing line remainder returning to Chateau ROSENTHAL	
9. p.m. 21 Feb	Bn left Chateau ROSENTHAL & proceeded to YPRES.	R.M.

Army Form C. 2118.

WAR DIARY
or
INTELLIGENCE SUMMARY.
(Erase heading not required.)

Instructions regarding War Diaries and Intelligence Summaries are contained in F.S. Regs., Part II, and the Staff Manual respectively. Title pages will be prepared in manuscript.

Hour, Date, Place.	Summary of Events and Information.	Remarks and references to Appendices.
22nd Feb.	The Battalion halted at YPRES.	P.H. part of FIFTH DIVn
7 AM 23 Feb.	The Batt proceeded I road to BAILLEUL (15 miles) on the Brigade coming under the orders of 5' Divn.	P.H.
23 Feb – 27 Feb.	Battalion halted at BAILLEUL. Battalion left BAILLEUL and marching via NEUVE EGLISE and WULVERGHEM took over the trenches from BEDFORD REGT. Head Quarters was established at ELBOW FM.	P.H.

Signed
A.H....
C.P. Checkwn

Gulab Singh & Sons, Calcutta—No. 22 Army C.—5·8·14—1,07,000.

Army Form C. 2118.

WAR DIARY
or
INTELLIGENCE SUMMARY.

(Erase heading not required.)

Instructions regarding War Diaries and Intelligence Summaries are contained in F.S. Regs., Part II, and the Staff Manual respectively. Title pages will be prepared in manuscript.

Hour, Date, Place.	Summary of Events and Information.	Remarks and references to Appendices.
24 Feby 1915	Distribution of Men in Trenches on 24th Feby on taking over from Bedford Regt. FIRING LINE – No 1 & 4 Coys RESERVES – a) R.E. FARM, and No 5 Support Tr. No 3 Coy. – 2) GABLE FARM – No 2 Coy	2/2

5th Div.
84th Bde.

WAR DIARY

2nd CHESHIRE REGT.

MARCH
1915.

Attached:-
Operation Orders.

WAR DIARY
or
INTELLIGENCE SUMMARY.
(Erase heading not required.)

Army Form C. 2118.

Place	Date	Hour	Summary of Events and Information	Remarks and references to Appendices
	March 1st 1915		FIRING LINE Coys were relieved by No. 2 + 3 Coys	was
	March 3rd 1915	4.15 PM	Capt Turner, L/Cpl Lloyd & Pte Wainwright No. 3 Coy, left trenches to reconnoitre a supposed GERMAN SAP. Subsequently the Coy was relieved by 1st Suffolk Regt and proceeded to BRIGADE RESERVE at BUS FARM - Two Not Coy which remained at BAZLE FARM, under orders of O/C SUFFOLK REGT. Capt. TURNER + 2 MEN not having returned were officially reported missing.	was
	March 5th 1915	6 PM	The BN discovered Coy left billets to improve trenches and dig new ones 1 Coy 1st MONMOUTH Regt was placed under orders of O/C to assist.	was was
	March 4th 1915	2 AM	The BN returned to billets.	was
	March 7th 1915	4.45 PM	The BN left BUS FARM to proceed to BAILLEUL to come into ARMY RESERVE.	was
	March 7th 1915	11 PM	The BN arrived at BAILLEUL.	was
BAILLEUL	March 8 " " 9 " " 10 "		BN remained in ARMY RESERVE " " " " " " " " " " " "	was was was was

WAR DIARY
or
INTELLIGENCE SUMMARY.
(Erase heading not required.)

Army Form C. 2118.

Instructions regarding War Diaries and Intelligence Summaries are contained in F. S. Regs., Part II, and the Staff Manual respectively. Title pages will be prepared in manuscript.

Hour, Date, Place.	Summary of Events and Information.	Remarks and references to Appendices.
10 am 11th March 1915 BAILLEUL	A draft of 2 Officers (Capt Routh and Lieut Smith) and 200 other ranks arrived from England	was
12:30 am 11th March " "	Orders received to march at 11 PM to R.E farm to take part in operations in conjunction with 7th Brigade. The Bn was divided as under:- 2 Coys (Nos 1 and 2) to carry out the attack under the Comdg Officer. 2 Coys (No.s 3 and 4) to remain in Reserve in R.E farm under Major Stone, under the orders of the Brigadier. Owing to the attack by the 7th Brigade having failed, the Bn was not ordered to launch its attack. During the operation No.s 1 & 2 Coys were heavily shelled. Casualties :- 1 Officer (Lt/T.H.M. CHAPLIN) wounded. Other ranks :- 3 killed, 10 wounded, 1 missing.	was 7/2 z
10-3:30 PM 13th March NOUVERGE	Bn received orders to return to billets at BAILLEUL	was
5-15 PM 13th March BAILLEUL	Bn arrived at BAILLEUL	was
6-am 14th March " "	Orders received to march southwards and take over 10th Bgd area.	was
3- PM 14th March PETIT PONT	Bn left BAILLEUL and marched to Petit Pont Farm.	was
9- PM 14th March " "	Orders received to march to ROMARIN to billets	was
2:30 am 15th March ROMARIN	Bn arrived at ROMARIN	was
10 PM 15th March ROMARIN	Bn marched to PIGGERIES and Grand Munque farms, in BRIGADE RESERVE.	
2:30 am 16 March PLOEGSTEERT	Bn arrived PLOEGSTEERT.	was
16 " "	Bn in Brigade Reserve.	was
12-30 PM 17 " "	Bn marched to BAILLEUL and arrived at 5 PM in Army Reserve	was
" 18 " BAILLEUL	Bn in Army Reserve	was
4 PM " "	Orders received to KEMMEL to relieve 7th Brigade.	was

Army Form C. 2118.

WAR DIARY
or
INTELLIGENCE SUMMARY.
(Erase heading not required.)

Instructions regarding War Diaries and Intelligence Summaries are contained in F. S. Regs., Part II, and the Staff Manual respectively. Title pages will be prepared in manuscript.

Hour, Date, Place.		Summary of Events and Information.	Remarks and references to Appendices.
7 A.M. 19 March	BAILLEUL	Orders received to relieve 4 S. Lancs R & 2 S. Lancs R in Sector F. DRANOUTRE Section.	Brigade O.O. No 14 Reg: O.O. No 15.
4 P.M. " "	"	Bn. moved off to trenches.	
10.25 P.M. "	KEMMEL	Relief complete. Head Quarters established at the CHALET - KEMMEL	2/22 R.H.
12 noon 20 "	KEMMEL	Casualties previous 24 hours No 1. 1 killed 2 wounded	R.H.
6.30 P.M. "	"	Ration convoy arrived - no 3+4 Coys relieved nos 1+2 Coys 2 Lieut IVENS + ROBERTS joined Bn from reported arrival. Brigadier Gen. visited trenches.	R.O.O 15.A
12 noon 21 "	KEMMEL	Casualties previous 24 hours No 1. 1 wounded	R.H.
7.15 P.M. "	"	Ration convoy arrived. Nos 1+2 Companies relieved Nos 3+4 companies	R.O.O 16
12 noon 22 "	KEMMEL	Casualties previous 24 hours No 2 - 2 wounded - 3 + 1 - - 4 - 2 - } Total 5.	R.H.
"	"	Ration convoy arrived. Nos 3 + 4 Companies + 1 platoon each N°s 1+2 Companies relieved Nos 1+2 Companies G.C. Support R. & 2 Co. officers also 2 cadets O.T.C. visited trenches.	R.O.O. 17 Co. 2 Lt. 24th K.3. W.14.
7.15 P.M. "	"		
12 noon 23 "	KEMMEL	Casualties previous 24 hours No 1. 0 killed 1 wounded - 2 - " 3 " - 3 - " 0 " - 4.1 " 2 " } Total 2 killed 6 wounded	R.H. R. O.O 18
7.45 P.M. "	"	Ration convoy arrived. Nos 1+2 Coys + 1 platoon each 3+4 Coys relieving Nos 3+4 Coys O.T.C. visited trenches.	R.H.

Gulab Singh & Sons, Calcutta—No. 22 Army C.£G.8.14—1,07,000.

WAR DIARY
or
INTELLIGENCE SUMMARY.

(Erase heading not required.)

Army Form C. 2118.

Instructions regarding War Diaries and Intelligence Summaries are contained in F.S. Regs., Part II, and the Staff Manual respectively. Title pages will be prepared in manuscript.

Hour, Date, Place.			Summary of Events and Information.	Remarks and references to Appendices.
12 noon	24 March	KEMMEL	Casualties previous 24 hours. N.O 4: – 1 Killed 2 wounded.	R.O.O. 19.
11.30 PM	24 March	KEMMEL	Casualties from 12 noon to 11.30 PM {N03 – 1 killed No 2 – 1 wounded	R O O 19.
11–30 PM	24 March	KEMMEL	Bn relieved by 1st Suffolk Regt.	2/2
12 noon	25 March	DRANOUTRE	2.30am. Billetted in huts & farms. H.Q. & Cos. Coote LEURIDAN	
12 noon	26 March	"	Bn in Brigade Reserve.	
5–15 PM	26 March	"	150 men each from Nos 1 – 3 – 4 Coys working party. Ammn trenches & lectrn. Casualties during working. { No 2 – 2 wounded No 3 – 1 wounded.	
12 noon	27 March	"	Bn in Brigade Reserve DRANOUTRE.	
9 am	28th March	"	Bn recd orders to relieve 1st Suffolk Regt in lectr F. DRANOUTRE Section	
6.20 PM	28th March	"	Bn moved off to Trenches. 6 Platoons "The Rangers" attached to Bn for trench duty.	R.O.O 20.
11–PM	28th March	LINDENHOEK	Relief completed. HE Qrs established at LINDENHOEK CHATEAU. Nos 3 & 4 Coys + 1 Platoon Rgt Trenches.	Cas 25th–28th K. W. 3
12 noon	29 March	"	Casualties previous 24 hours. 1 man the Rangers wounded.	
4 PM	29 March	"	Ration convoy arrived. Nos 1 and 2 Coys relieved. Nos 3 and 4 Coys, 3 Platoons Rangers remaining other 3 Platoons for instruction for 24 hours.	R.O.O 21
12 noon	30 March	"	4 Students from Cadet School Bailleul attached for instruction with convoy.	
7–10 PM	30 March	"	Casualties previous 24 hours: 1 man wounded. The man the Rangers Killed. Ration party arrived with convoy. Nos 3 + 4 + 3 Platoons Rangers relieved 1 + 2 Coys and 3 Platoons Rangers	R O O 22.
11–PM	30 march	"	3 Platoons each of No. 1 and 2 Coys handed in fatigues in trenches etc. This party returned to Bn Reserve about 3 am 31-3-15.	
12 noon	31 March	"	Casualties previous 24 hours. No 2 – 2 men wounded. Rangers 1 man wounded.	Cas 29–31st K.O.W. 3 W 1+20
4 PM	31 March	"	French Cavalier notified that no relief would take place tonight.	MK 7
6 am	1 April	"	Bn received order that relief would take place tonight.	M 1 + 3
12 noon	"	"	Casualties 12 noon 31 March – 6 wounded	
11–PM	"	"	Bn relieved by 1st Suffolk Regt & proceeded to billets at DRANOUTRE	

OPERATION ORDERS.

2.Ches.R. O.O. No 15.
19.3.16.

Ref. map 1/20000 . 1/40000 No 28.

1. The Bn will take over trenches of 4 S. LANCS R. To-night.
2. Parade so as to pass Bn starting point in following order at 3.50 p.m.
    No 1. 2. 3. 4. M.G. Sect?. Transport - as ordered.
  Route. DRANOUTRE - LINDENHOEK GUARD - LINDENHOEK cross roads - KEMMEL.
3. Tea will be issued as near LINDENHOEK GUARD.
4. Transport will move as under.
(a) At 1 P.M. Cooks carts) to Tea place.
            Water carts) Coy. Q. M. Serjt. & cooks per Coy to accompany.

(b) With Bn. Toll carts.
            M.G. wagons.
            Maxim cart

(c) To Transport billets area Remainder of Transport. direct. (M 34 d 2.8)

5. Companies will be distributed as under
  No 1 Coy. F 3   Rifles 12
            F 4   -   50 } 2/2. 1 M.G.
            F 5   - 150 }   1 M.G.

  No 2 Coy F 6   -   50
           F 7   -   50
           Sup? Pt 2 - 50 1 officer 1 M.G.
            " " 3 - 50 1 officer 1 M.G.

  Nos 3 & 4 Coys - in KEMMEL S' of LA CLYTTE - WYTSCHAETE Road.
  Hd Qrs and M.O. KEMMEL CHALET.

6. At the Tea place, rations will be taken off the carts and the latter will be distributed to Nos 1 & 2 Coys.
Then tools as Bn property must be handed over nightly & brought out of the trenches by the Companies leaving them on completion of tour of duty of the Battalion.
There may be also in the trenches

F 3.	1 pick.	2 shovels
F 4 }	8 -	36 -
F 5 }		
F 6	5 -	15 -
F 7	4 -	12.

7. O.C. 3 & 4 companies will detail 1 officer + NCO to visit the trenches & supporting points occupied by Nos 2 & 1 respectively. They will afterwards return to their billets.

8. Coys in the fire trenches will be relieved nightly taking rations & water bottles filled into the trenches.

9. Guides will meet Nos 1 & 2 companies at LINDEN cross roads at 7.15 p.m.

Regimental orderlies will accompy parties
   Pte WAKEFIELD into F3. F4 F5.
   - BROCKLEHURST - F6
   - MONT - F7
   - DAVIS - Sup: pt No 2.
   - EDMONDS - - No 3.

Pte WAKEFIELD will report to Capt. MORTON upon leaving the Tea place. Remainder will report to Capt HUGHES at the same place.
Issued at 1 p.m.

R. Shuter
Adjt 2 Lancs R

2 Ches R.O. No 1½

21.3.15

Relief of Trenches will be carried out to night as follows

```
To  F2.   1 Platoon No 3 p. n. S.P. No 2
    F3.   18.12 men No 2.
    F4 )  Remainder No 2
    F5 )  30 men   No 1
    F6    20 men   No 1.
    F7    50 men   No 1
    S.P.2 50 men   No 1
    S.P.3 30 men   No 1.
```

Order of March

```
No 2. Coy to F3. F4. F5.      ) M.G. rations - 2 detachments
                              ) 1000 sand bags
                              ) 1 Box Verrey pistol ammunition
No 1 Coy. 30 men to F4 F5 )    24 rifle grenades.
                               80 floor boards
                                                    rations
1 Coy 50 men  S.P. No 2    M.G. sect rations, 50 men No 3
-  20 men to F6            1 Tin chloride lime.
-  50  -  - F 7
-  50  "  - S.P.3          1 M.G Rations
```

Issued in under 2 p.m.
```
No 1   C.O. No 1
   2    -  No 2
   3    C.O
   4    Capt. Stone
   5    Machine Gun Officer
```

R Shirley
Adj. 2/the R.

2 Ches Regt. O.O. No 17
22. 3. 15.

1 Relief of trenches will be carried out
To-night as under
   To F2   75 men No 3 Cy & 1 M.G.
  " F3   12 men No 3 Coy
  " F4 } No 4 Coy and 2 M.G.
  " F5 }
  " F6   1 Platoon No 3 Coy.
  " F7   1 Platoon No 1 Coy
  " S2   1 "   " 3 Coy (Lt Ward)
  " S3   1 "   " 2 Coy.
  KEMMEL No 1 Coy less 1 platoon
          No 2 " " 1 "

Issued 6.15 p.m.

R Hurley
Adjutant
2/Cheshire Regt

2nd Class R. O O No 18
23. 3. 15.

1. Reliefs to-night will be as under.
   No 1. Coy.
   F 2   75 men   Capt. MORTON.
   F 3   12 -   N.C.O.
   F 6   50 -   1 officer
   S.P.2 50 -   1 officer (from F7)

   No 2 Coy
   F4. F5.   Whole Company

   No 3 Coy
   F7   50 men   1 officer (from F6)
         150 -   Bn Resrv KEMMEL.

   No 4 Coy
   S.P.3 50 men   1 officer.
          150 men   Bn Reserve KEMMEL.

   Rations & water for these will be brought up
   on pack animals & placed behind farm on
   LINDENHOEK ROAD S of S.P.3
   After relieving - small parties will be sent to take
   their rations & water.
   Officers Commanding Nos 1 & 4 will send 2 men
   to unload & take charge of their rations.

   Issued 12.30 p.m.   R. H. —— Capt.
                                    Adjutant & Chief R.

General work to be done in accordance with G. O's
orders are.
(1) The extension of Trench from F2 - F4 and from
    F4 - F2 in order to make one continuous
    trench and evacuate No 3 Trench.
(2) A complete system of communicating Trenches
    from the Supporting points to support trenches
    and from the support trenches to the fire trenches
    Officers commanding corps in the trenches and
    officers commanding units in supporting points
    & support trenches will send in a rough sketch
    of their posts and will report at 4 AM to-morrow
    showing to what extent the above has been
    carried out and giving the exact length of
    work done.

1 Bn. Cheshire Regt. Operation Order No 17
24-3-1915

1. The Battn will move to DRANOUTRE this evening after being relieved by the Suffolk Regt.

2. Companies (when complete) will march independently to their billets.
Platoons in S.P.2, S.P.3, F.6, F.3, and F.4 will rejoin their companies on relief on ground near bandstand at KEMMEL
Commanders of parties returning to KEMMEL will at once report to Adjt at Bn. Head Qrs.

3. Officers Commanding Companies will report their occupation of billets at DRANOUTRE to Bn Hd Qrs there

4. At 6-30 pm tonight 3 Platoons of Nos 3 & 4 Coys will parade with rifles & ammunition but without packs and carry the following to the farm on LINDENHOCK ROAD near supporting point No 3

Stores to be carried by each Company
Ammunition 28 boxes
Biscuit Tins 9
Quicklime Bags 1
Sandbags 2000

5. Battn Hd Qrs at DRANOUTRE will be at Estaminet on N Side of Lower DRANOUTRE - BAILLEUL ROAD.

Issued at 4 pm. (Sgd) A. R. Hill Capt
24-3-1915   & Adjt of Cheshire Regt.

R. OO 2? / 29. 3-15

Garrison for night 29/30 March 1915

- F5 } N° 1 C° Cheshire Regt
- F4 } 3 Platoons The Rangers (less 50 men & 1 officer)
- F2. 2 Platoons N° 2 C°
- F6. 50 men & 1 officer N° 2 C°
- SP2 50 men & 1 officer N° 2 C°
- SP3. 50 men & 1 officer The Rangers.

Work to be done tonight

F5. Construction of Trench from L.P. & Barricade on LINDEN HOEK
  (a) Road. Draining & reveting with Sand bags
  (b) Improvement of parapet & Traverses where required
  Making of panados especially in places where
  enfilade fire can be brought to bear from enemy's
  Trenches to front & R of C Section

F4. Draining & improvement of Communication trench between
  F4 & F6.
  Improvement of parapet & Traverses

F6. Draining & improvement of Communication Trenches from
  between F6 to F4 & SP2

F2. Completion & revetment of parapet in continuation
  towards E2 & F4

SP3. Assist R.E. in making dug outs inside Redoubt

SP2 So assist R.E. when required —

R 00 22 17 30-3-15

Garrison of Trenches - 30/31 March 1915

F2. 2 Platoons N° 3 C°

F6 1 Platoon N° 3 C°

SP2 1 Platoon N° 3 C°

F.4 } N° 4 C°
F.5 } 3 Platoons The Rangers (less 50 men & 1 offr)

~~F6~~
SP3 50 men & 1 officer The Rangers

—— Work to be done ——

F2 (1) Continue revetment of parapet lriads E²
   (2)   "   "   "   "   lriads F4
        and build Firing Platforms.
   (3). Make Parados - with Trench Boxes.

F4. (a) So necessary work inside Fire Trenches
    (b) Widen & deepen where required Communication
        Trench to F6

F5. (1) Continue revetment of beluise on of Trench to
        Barricade under supervision of R.E.
    (2) Necessary work inside Fire Trench
    (3) Build Parados with Trench Boxes

F6 (a). Level & straighten parapet on the right
    (b) Drain widen & deepen Communication Trenches to
        SP 2 and F4.

SP2 (a) Finish communication Trench to new M Gun Emplacement
    (b) Assist R E in finishing dug outs
SP3 - Assist R E in finishing dug outs

Regtl OO No 22 of 30-3-15

1. The Battn will furnish working parties tonight as under:-

    a. Party to parade at Dug-out behind SP2 after being relieved.
    Capt P.G. Villiers-Stuart
    1 Platoon No 2 from SP.2.
    1 Platoon No 2 from F.6.   } Diggers.
    1 Platoon Rangers from SP.3.
    1 Platoon Rangers from F.4.
    Cooks for this party will make tea behind SP.2. and will parade with camp kettles, groceries etc, at LINDENHOEK cross roads, at 4-15 PM.

    b. Under Captain E.L. Morton for fatigue carrying tools, laying floorboards, etc. from SPY FARM:-
    3 Platoons No 1 Coy.
    1 Platoon No 2 Coy.
    "b" party to march to billets and have tea.
    Parade LINDENHOEK cross roads 11 PM.
    Marching order, greatcoat, without packs.

    c. To remain in Battn Reserve in billets on relief:-
    1 Platoon No 1 Coy
    1 Platoon No 2 Coy
    1 Platoon "Rangers."

    Howard Arter Maj
    1/Cheshire Regt

28th Div.

84th Bde.

Note:- 84th Bde rejoined 28 Div
from 5th Div. on 6th Apl.

WAR DIARY.

2nd CHESHIRE REGT.

APRIL

1915.

Army Form O. 2118.

WAR DIARY
or
INTELLIGENCE SUMMARY.
(Erase heading not required.)

Instructions regarding War Diaries and Intelligence Summaries are contained in F. S. Regs., Part II, and the Staff Manual respectively. Title pages will be prepared in manuscript.

Hour, Date, Place.	Summary of Events and Information.	Remarks and references to Appendices.
6 am 1st April DRANOUTRE LINDENHOEK	By received orders that relief would take place tonight	was was was was
12 noon 1st April " "	Casualties to 12 noon — No 3 Coy 6 men wounded by their fire.	
11 PM 1st April " "	B" relieved by 1st Suffolks and proceeded to billets at DRANOUTRE	
12 noon 2 April DRANOUTRE	B" returned to billets at DRANOUTRE and placed in Divisional Reserve. The following copy of letter received by Commdg Officer from O.C. 1st Wiltshire Regt was published in Battn Orders with reference to the Gallant Conduct of Sergt WYNNE and Pte BEDDA:—	was

"To the O/C 2" CHESHIRE Regt.

" Thank you very much for sending the effects of the late Recruit Hooper. Will you please convey to SERGT WYNNE, and PTE BEDDA my deep appreciation of and high admiration for their very gallant conduct in bringing in this Officers body. My Battn thoroughly understand the great trouble risk that this N.C.O. and man ran for which they cannot too highly thank them and desire to place on record their sense of their obligations to them for their great heroism.

WAR DIARY
INTELLIGENCE SUMMARY

Army Form C. 2118.

Hour, Date, Place.	Summary of Events and Information.	Remarks and references to Appendices.
April		
DRANOUTRE 2. noon. 2nd April 1915.	B:N returned to billets at DRANOUTRE 1.30 a.m. and placed in IIIVN RESERVE.	was
" 12. noon 3rd April 1915	B:N in IIIVN RESERVE.	was
" 4. P.M. 3rd April 1915	B:N marched to BAILLEUL to BILLETS and placed in ARMY RESERVE arrived in billets 4-40 P.M. H:Q:rs established R:ue-de-la-GARE.	was
"	The following complimentary order was published in R.O. of this date:— R.O.B. N:o 4-4-15	
"	The G.O.C. 5th Division has expressed to G.O.C. 84th B:g:de his high appreciation of the splendid work which has been carried out by all the B:n:s of the 84th Brigade especially taking into consideration the very habile time the Brigade had at YPRES.	
"	The G.O.C. Division also wrote to express regret that the 84th Brigade has been taken from his Command. He wishes it to be known that he is reporting most favourably on the 84th Brigade to G.O.C. 28th Division which the Brigade is about to join and through him to the G.O.C. of the Army Corps with a view to the report being communicated to G.O.C. in Chief of the British Army in the Field.	
"	These complimentary remarks were expressed verbally by G.O.C. 84th Brigade to the Officer Com:d:g; who has the greatest pleasure and satisfaction in communicating them to all ranks of the Bat:n	
BAILLEUL. 4.PM 4th April 1915	B:N in Army Reserve	was
" 1. P.M 5 April 1915	B:N in Army Reserve.	was
" 3 P.M 6 April 1915	B:N placed under the orders of 28th DIVISION. (with 84th Brigade)	was
6 April 1915	Army Q—5-8-14—1,07,000 Lieut. Carter joined	was

Army Form C. 2118.

WAR DIARY
or
INTELLIGENCE SUMMARY.
(Erase heading not required.)

Instructions regarding War Diaries and Intelligence Summaries are contained in F. S. Regs., Part II, and the Staff Manual respectively. Title pages will be prepared in manuscript.

Hour, Date, Place.	Summary of Events and Information.	Remarks and references to Appendices.
3 P.M. 6th April BAILLEUL	Orders were that B/H Bgde were re-transferred to 28th Div. from the 1st Army (was)	
12 noon 7th April " "	Bⁿ paraded for inspection of Bgde by G.O.C 2nd Army (General Sir H Smith-Dorrien.) was	
3 PM 8th April " "	All men who arrived as drafts since 1st March, inspected by G.O.C. 8th A. Brigade. was	
8th April " "	The following report from G.O.C. 5th Div, K.G.O.C. 5th Corps was circulated to Units in 8th A. Bgde. (Confidential).	R.O.O. No 23. 8/4/14.
	"On the departure of the 83rd and 84th Brigades from the 5th DIVISION I wish to place on record my appreciation of the excellent work they have done since they have been with it. They arrived somewhat weak after experiencing a hard time near YPRES but they soon received large drafts and have tackled the work in the trenches in a very thorough manner. Well commanded, well officered and well disciplined all ranks have worked with a will. I am sure that today there are no finer Brigades in the Expeditionary Force."	
	— Bⁿ inspected by G.O.C 5th Corps (Lt Gen. Sir H. Plumer.)	
9.10 A.M. 11th April " "	Bⁿ marched to VLAMERTINGHE to rejoin 28th DIV^N.	
3.20 PM " "	Bⁿ arrived & were placed in billets. H.Q^{rs} established at VLAMERTINGHE	
10 am 12 April " VLAMERTINGHE	Bⁿ resting.	
6 PM. " "		
13.14.15th April " "		
5 PM 15 Apl " "	Bⁿ proceeded to ZONEBEEKE via YPRES to relieve 8th Bⁿ M/adloses in trenches, taken over by 84th Brigade from this date	R.O.O No 24 15/4/13

Gulab Singh & Sons, Calcutta—No. 22 Army C.—5-8-14—1,07,000.

Army Form C. 2118.

WAR DIARY
or
INTELLIGENCE SUMMARY.
(Erase heading not required.)

Hour, Date, Place.	Summary of Events and Information.	Remarks and references to Appendices.
2 AM 16 April 1915 ZONNEBEKE	Trench relief completed. Battn occupying right sector of Brigade line. Name of "A" Sector - 1 - 2 - 3. Trench Garrison distributed as under:-	
	Trench "A"1 - No 1 Coy 200 rifles.	
	"A" 2 - No 2 Coy 200 rifles. } Bn H.Qrs - Farm MOLENAARELSTHOEK
	"A" 3 - No 3 Coy 200 rifles.	
	Supports - No 4 Coy 200 rifles	
12 noon 16 April. MOLENAARELSTHOEK	Casualties to 12 noon - 2 other ranks killed - 3 wounded	
12 noon 17th April " "	Casualties to 12 noon - 3 other ranks killed - 4 wounded	
11 PM 17th April " "	Battn relieved by 12th Suffolk Regt; and proceeded to Brigade Reserve.	
2.30 am 18 April ST JEAN	Bn arrived at ST JEAN (less No 1 & 4 Coys). Bn H.Qrs established at Pté	
	No 1 & 4 Coys under Capt Roach billeted at Wieme Mills YPRES.	
19 April " "	Bn in Brigade Reserve. Or apt of 1 offr & 36 men arrived (for Chaplains)	
20 April " "	Bn in Brigade Reserve. 1 Offr & 30 men detailed to take ober to trenches.	L/Cpl. P.C. Montonhy joined
2-30 PM 20 April " "	1st Suffolk Regt in trenches, night 21-22nd April	
1.30 PM 21 April " "	Orders received to relieve 1st Suffolk Regt in trenches, night 21-22nd April	
2-0 PM 22 April " "	Orders received that trench relief for 21-22 April cancelled.	
	The "Bn" was called out to support 1st Suffolk Regt at 2.0 p.m. owing to	
	a heavy German attack on left in which asphyxiating gas was	
	used on the Ger: trenches against us. Bn: lay in field in	*N-21*
	enclos: behind FREZENBURG all afternoon.	
	15 men were wounded by shell fire	*N-22*
	Shelf cancelled.	
23 April FREZENBURG	In support behind FREZENBURG	
10 am 23 April ZONNEBEKE	Rejoined 1st Bn Suffolk Regt. Head Qrs established at MOLARENVESTHOEK No.1 and 4 Coys in trenches No. 2 and 3 in Support	*N-28*

Gulab Singh & Sons, Calcutta—No. 22 Army C.—5-8-14—1,07,000.

WAR DIARY
or
INTELLIGENCE SUMMARY.
(Erase heading not required.)

Army Form C. 2118.

Instructions regarding War Diaries and Intelligence Summaries are contained in F. S. Regs., Part II, and the Staff Manual respectively. Title pages will be prepared in manuscript.

Hour, Date, Place.	Summary of Events and Information.	Remarks and references to Appendices.
24th April ZONNEBEKE	In trenches 1 and 2 of B.2. No 2 and 3 in trenches (casualties 3 men killed, 11 wounded)	
25 April "	Heavily shelled and turned out. All trenches lost. Had to bang-moved into adjacent dug outs.	(casualties 6.0.g. 3 men killed 12 wounded)
26 April ZONNEBEKE 3 pm.	Batt: remained in trenches. During this time met to following casualties occurred. 16 men killed. Capt: Walbrook. 2 Lieut Pedding (wounded). Lieut A Barros and 79 o.Ranks wounded. 2 Lieut: Sams & Butler attached to 10th. Royal S Fusb (from Zillebeke) 23 o.Ranks missing	
10 am May ZONNEBEKE	The Batt: took line of troops occupying the YPRES Salient was withdrawn to a fresh line of trenches in order made the retirement menaced this movement. In the trenches occupied by the Battalion at ZONNEBEKE, Captain Officers Vincent & Hardman, with 30 other ranks remained in occupation to cover the withdrawal of the Battalion which was carried out without any casualties. The new line of trenches running just East of FREZENBURG	

Gulab Singh & Sons, Calcutta—No. 32 Army C.—5-8-14—1,07,000.

28th Div.
84th Bde.

WAR DIARY.

2nd CHESHIRE REGT.

MAY

1 9 1 5.

Army Form C. 2118.

WAR DIARY
or
INTELLIGENCE SUMMARY.
(Erase heading not required.)

Instructions regarding War Diaries and Intelligence Summaries are contained in F. S. Regs., Part II. and the Staff Manual respectively. Title pages will be prepared in manuscript.

Place	Date	Hour	Summary of Events and Information	Remarks and references to Appendices
ZONNEBEKE	26th April to 3rd May		Battalion remained in trenches. During this period the following casualties occurred :- 16 men killed, Captain Mallinson, Captain Villiers Stuart, 2nd Lieut. McSwiney, 2nd Lieut. Alderson and 79 other ranks wounded. 2nd Lieuts. Ivens & Rutter admitted to hospital (shocky from shell fire) 23 other ranks missing.	
	4th May 10.p.m.	"	The whole line of troops occupying the YPRES Salient was withdrawn to the fresh line of trenches in order to make the salient much less pronounced. In the trenches occupied by the Battalion at ZONNEBEKE. One officer (Lieut. Newman) with 30 other ranks remained in occupation to cover the withdrawal of the Battalion which was carried out without any casualties. The new line of trenches running just East of FREZENBURG	

continued on next page

Army Form C. 2118.

WAR DIARY
or
INTELLIGENCE SUMMARY.
(Erase heading not required.)

Instructions regarding War Diaries and Intelligence Summaries are contained in F. S. Regs., Part II, and the Staff Manual respectively. Title pages will be prepared in manuscript.

Hour, Date, Place.	Summary of Events and Information.	Remarks and references to Appendices.
5 May. POTIJZE	were eventually to following other units 1st Suffolks 1 Suffolks Regt, 1 Welch Regt, 1 Monmouth Regt.	H.Q.
5-6 May POTIJZE	The Battalion now occupied the trenches dug out on the	H.Q.
9 am 6 May POTIJZE	G.H.Q. moves to POTIJZE. Casualties 28 other ranks wounded Battalion remained in support trenches.	
7 May "	Major A.J. Stone assumed command from vice Lieut Col Ernest Gore-Elwood on so to that. Capt. S.C. South killed.	H.Q.
"	No 1 and 4 Co.s were detailed to support the 1st Welch Regt on the firing line. Battalion Head Qrs moved to mound farm in Square C. 29. b. 6. 8. (sheet 28 North) Casualties Other ranks 20 men and 6 men killed, 7 other ranks wounded.	H.Q.
11 pm 7 May. VERLORENHOEK	No 1 and 4 Coys took over the section of the firing line held by 1st Welsh Regt. No 2 and 3 Co's occupying the support trenches.	H.Q.
7 May "	Casualties- Six men killed Capt. V.S. Will and 7 men wounded. WILL	H.Q.

WAR DIARY or INTELLIGENCE SUMMARY

Hour, Date, Place.	Summary of Events and Information.	Remarks and references to Appendices.
8 May. VERLORENHOEK	A heavy bombardment of the trenches was commenced by the enemy about daybreak and was carried on incessantly until the line was broken to a finer Infantry attack made with overwhelming numbers. Notwithstanding the heavy resist[ance] by the enemy. The battalions overwhelmed by the Bat[talio]n Hd Qrs and Coy 1 and 4 of B.C. were surrounded by the enemy and with very few exceptions the whole of the officers (including Major Stone Comdg Offer and Capt Marq Col Ox) and other ranks were killed or taken prisoners. The following casualties occurred that day:— Killed. 17 other ranks. Wounded. 1 Lieut Newman, Lieut. Lieut Thompson, Hughes and 200 other ranks. Missing. Major Lowe, Capt. Hayes Newington, Lieut Nash, Lieut Hayes Newington, Newington, Rickard, Washington, Stewart and Claldin and 182 other ranks (including Regt Sgt Major Nant.)	

WAR DIARY
or
INTELLIGENCE SUMMARY.
(Erase heading not required.)

Army Form C. 2118.

Instructions regarding War Diaries and Intelligence Summaries are contained in F. S. Regs., Part II, and the Staff Manual respectively. Title pages will be prepared in manuscript.

Hour, Date, Place.	Summary of Events and Information.	Remarks and references to Appendices.
8. May. VERLORENHOEK	After the attack of the enemy, the firing line was reinforced in what had hitherto been the support trenches. About 500 yards in rear of original trenches. Of the two officers (Lieuts T. Roberts and T. S. Nevell) and the other ranks remaining, two were put under the command of Lt-Col. L. O. W. Jordan. Comdg. 1/Gr. Nrth. L. Regt. that Battalion being also in occupation of the ⟨…⟩ a portion of the new firing line.	D.S.3
9. May. VERLOREN HOEK	The Battalion under Lieut Roberts remained in trenches - a heavy bombardment by the enemy was continued throughout the day. A draft from England consisting of 3 N.C.Os. and 3. J. Nicholson and 216 other ranks arrived at Eurrgfort Camp East of POPERINGHE and A.D.C. Meadows joined on first reinforcement.	D.S.6
11 am 10 May. VERLORENHOEK	Orders received from Brigade to collect all available men with stragglers from trenches in readiness to go into trenches. Officers & staff, with stragglers from trenches, and supplied men	

Army Form C. 2118.

WAR DIARY
or
INTELLIGENCE SUMMARY.

(Erase heading not required.)

Instructions regarding War Diaries and Intelligence Summaries are contained in F. S. Regs., Part II, and the Staff Manual respectively. Title pages will be prepared in manuscript.

Hour, Date, Place.	Summary of Events and Information.	Remarks and references to Appendices.
7 a.m. 10 May VERLORENHOEK	Formed into two Cos (A and B) under Lieut-Jefferson and Nicholson respectively. The whole being under command of Lieut S.C. Esson	J.C.
7.15 a.m. 10 May "	Orders received from Brigade for details reference above to proceed from transport lines East of POPERINGHE to join remainder of Battalion in trenches immediately	J.C.
" "	Details (as above moved off as directed and on arrival at level crossing (Sq. H.11. d 6 or 28. ......) in motor lorries (motor buses) reserve of Battalion in Rest near S. of YPRES so remainder of Battalion in trenches was being relieved. Huts occupied	J.C.
11 a.m. 10 May YPRES	Remainder of Bn from trenches under Lieut G. Roberts joined details of Bn in rest.	J.C.

Gulab Singh & Sons, Calcutta—No. 22 Army C.—5-8-14—1,07,000.

Army Form C. 2118.

WAR DIARY
or
INTELLIGENCE SUMMARY.
(Erase heading not required.)

Instructions regarding War Diaries and Intelligence Summaries are contained in F.S. Regs., Part II, and the Staff Manual respectively. Title pages will be prepared in manuscript.

Hour, Date, Place.	Summary of Events and Information.	Remarks and references to Appendices.
11 May / YPRES	Battalion remained in rest. Capt. C.P. Rushout assumed command.	J.E.
5 pm 11 May / "	Batt. moved to huts near POPERINGHE in SE G.3. Sect. 28 H/000. Composite Battalion was formed consisting of 2 Cheshire Regt, 2 Northumberland Fus., 1 Suffolk Regt, 1 Monmouth Regt, 7th under the command of Major P.J. Yorke, Monmouth Regt.	J.E.
12 May POPERINGHE	Battalion remained in huts.	J.E.
6 pm 12 " / "	Battalion (with remainder of composite Batt.) marched to LILLE [at. BOENHAERT] 3 m. S. of POPERINGHE	J.E.
13 May BOENHAERT	In billets	J.E.
4 am 14 May / "	Battalion (2 Cheshire) marched to BRANDHOEK (S.G.6.d.) Sect. 28 H/000 and remained billeted here in huts & tarpaulins.	J.E.
15-18 May BRANDHOEK	Remained in billets.	J.E.
10.20 am 19 May / "	Battalion bivouacked by road to HERZEELE and occupied billets there. Amalgamation of four units into a composite Battalion discontinued. Command of Battalion re-assumed by Capt. C.P. Rushout.	J.E.

Gulab Singh & Sons, Calcutta—No. 22 Army C.—5-8-14—1,07,000.

Army Form C. 2118.

WAR DIARY
or
INTELLIGENCE SUMMARY.

(Erase heading not required.)

Instructions regarding War Diaries and Intelligence Summaries are contained in F. S. Regs., Part II, and the Staff Manual respectively. Title pages will be prepared in manuscript.

Hour, Date, Place.	Summary of Events and Information.	Remarks and references to Appendices.
20 May. HERZEELE	In billets. Lieut N.J.A. Dawson and C.S. Edwards 3rd Canadian Bn. arrived.	
21 May -"-	In billets. Lieut. S.S. Scott and draft of 93 other ranks arrived.	
11 am 21 May -"-	Battalion (together with the other units of the 1st Bgde) were assembled in the Market Garden under the Brigade-Commander, Brig. Genl. R.E.W. Turner V.C., C.B., D.S.O. and were inspected by the Commander in Chief, Field Marshal Sir John French, G.C.B. &c. The C. in C. addressing the Brigade said — "I have come here today to see you 1st Brigade, every officer, N.C.O. and man, and personally thank you and express my admiration of the splendid work you have performed in which with no Staff & Reserves & no Supports, in what I shall call the Battle of St. Julien, you magnificent ..."	

Gulab Singh & Sons, Calcutta—No. 22 Army C—5-8-13—1,07,000.

WAR DIARY
or
INTELLIGENCE SUMMARY

Army Form C. 2118.

(Erase heading not required.)

Hour, Date, Place.	Summary of Events and Information.	Remarks and references to Appendices.
21 Aug. HERZEELE	Inspection— Fighting Ameublie and nearly. Though your losses are serious they have never heated the very wonderful spirit you have manifested during the recent heavy fighting against vastly superior numbers. You have endured non-countable losses. I am sorry for it, but your achievements have been great. During those trying days when the enemy ordered everyone in vain to break through your lines in order to reach the coast, the eyes of the world were on you. Had you not exercised the undaunted courage which you have exhibited in repelling him...	

Army Form C. 2118.

WAR DIARY
or
INTELLIGENCE SUMMARY.

(Erase heading not required.)

Instructions regarding War Diaries and Intelligence Summaries are contained in F. S. Regs., Part II, and the Staff Manual respectively. Title pages will be prepared in manuscript.

Hour, Date, Place.	Summary of Events and Information.	Remarks and references to Appendices.
22 May HERZEELE	Battalion to dig- and I trust the nature will recognise it as it is.	J.E.
23 May BRANDHOEK	Battalion moved to BRANDHOEK	J.E.
	Captain E.P. Garton, Colour E.P. Yaton, S/Sergt S.P. Yaton and Sergt R. McGregor arrived from England	J.E.
4 am 24 May — " —	Battalion called out. (Captain E.P. Garton-having assumed Command) and proceeded to [YPRES] following the J. railway line to ft town and Junctions Linsses in Square I 10. (Sheet 28) a position from which an attack was made on enemy's trenches about midnight. Battalion was suffered a withering rifle fire in the morning which drawing on from ground.	J.E.
11 am 25 May YPRES	Battalion retired and returned to BRANDHOEK having been relieved by 5 Cavalry Brigade.	J.E.

Gulab Singh & Sons, Calcutta—No. 22 Army C.—8-3-14—1,07,000.

Army Form C. 2118.

WAR DIARY
or
INTELLIGENCE SUMMARY.
(Erase heading not required.)

Instructions regarding War Diaries and Intelligence Summaries are contained in F.S. Regs., Part II, and the Staff Manual respectively. Title pages will be prepared in manuscript.

Hour, Date, Place.	Summary of Events and Information.	Remarks and references to Appendices.
24-25th May YPRES	The following casualties occurred in the Battalion during these two days :—	
	Killed :— 5 2nd Lieut Bacon, Roberts, Meecham, Dawson, McGuigan, and 8 other ranks.	
	Wounded :— 2 Colonel Barton and Major Lieut Cooke, 2nd Lieut Edwards, and 246 other ranks.	F.C.
	Missing :— 1 Capt. Andrews, and 25 other ranks.	
25th May BRAND HOEK	2nd Lieut S.B. Nelson assumed command of Battalion	F.C.
26-27 May "	Remained in billets	F.C.

Army Form C. 2118.

WAR DIARY
or
INTELLIGENCE SUMMARY.
(Erase heading not required.)

Instructions regarding War Diaries and Intelligence Summaries are contained in F. S. Regs., Part II, and the Staff Manual respectively. Title pages will be prepared in manuscript.

Hour, Date, Place.	Summary of Events and Information.	Remarks and references to Appendices.
11 a.m. 28/5/15 BRANDHOEK	Battalion marched to HERZEELE and occupied billets. New Captains S.O.S. Offrs. assumed command of Battalion. Marshalls Farm near Dorsetshire Regt	J.C.
12 noon 29/5/15 HERZEELE	The Battalion, together with the remnants of the 8th Brigade were accommodated in the Market Square, under the Brigade Comdr. (Brig Genl. Bols. in S. Summer). Billeting by the O.C. Comdr. (S. Bull. in S. Summer) Bn. to be completed Battalion in H.Q. Brigade. On the advance was H.Q. had performed Gardening during the excitement of the [illegible] Strength 1 offr. 3 offrs Carabine Regt and draft of 100 other ranks arrived	J.C. J.C. J.C.
30/5/15 – 2/6/15 HERZEELE 31 May " 3 June " 11 a.m. 3 June " 4 June	in billets. Being S.O.S. training. Battalion, together with remnants of the Kent Regt Draft in Yorks. Green in knowledge of the Yorkshire Draft. on Yorks Regts. 1st. the Yorks. [illegible] and L/Cpl Connor 3 Malcolm & joined [illegible] Lang Grenal and L.C. Connor	91 G.

28th Div.
84th Bde.

WAR DIARY.

2nd CHESHIRE REGT.

JUNE

1915.

Army Form C. 2118.

WAR DIARY
or
INTELLIGENCE SUMMARY.
(Erase heading not required.)

Instructions regarding War Diaries and Intelligence Summaries are contained in F. S. Regs., Part II. and the Staff Manual respectively. Title pages will be prepared in manuscript.

Place	Date	Hour	Summary of Events and Information	Remarks and references to Appendices
HERZEELE	30 May to 2 June		In billets	
	3 June	11 am	Battalion together with 8th Bgde paraded in review before in honour of His Majesty the King.	
	"			
	4 June		2 Lieuts R King-Smith and D.S.C Jones "Welshie R" joined	entered on next leaf

Army Form C. 2118.

WAR DIARY
or
INTELLIGENCE SUMMARY.

(Erase heading not required.)

Instructions regarding War Diaries and Intelligence Summaries are contained in F. S. Regs., Part II, and the Staff Manual respectively. Title pages will be prepared in manuscript.

Hour, Date, Place.	Summary of Events and Information.	Remarks and references to Appendices.
4-5th June HERZEELE	In Billets	J.G.
6 June — " —	2nd Lieut. R. Gordon 3rd Cheshire Regt. arrived with draft of 118 N. C. O's and men. together with Capt S. R. Barlow and Lieut E. L. Cross rejoining from hospital.	J.G.
" "	Night-alarm (Practice)	J.G.
11am 7 June		J.G.
8 June — " —	Battalion exercise at WYLDER in manning trenches and relieving trench garrisons. 2/Lt W.B. Bennetts R.E. rejoined Captain Barlow and Lieut Cross to hospital	J.G.
5am 9 June — " —	Gregns. route march. Command of Battalion assumed by Cr. Major B. Ramsden Conf Webb Ordered Join	J.G.
	Cotton P.O.Q Bttn who rejoined Yarmouth Bg.	J.G.
10 June — " —	In Billets	J.G.
2am 11 June — " —	Battalion ordered to RENINGHELST & now billeted.	J.G.

Army Form C. 2118.

WAR DIARY
or
INTELLIGENCE SUMMARY.
(Erase heading not required.)

Instructions regarding War Diaries and Intelligence Summaries are contained in F. S. Regs., Part II, and the Staff Manual respectively. Title pages will be prepared in manuscript.

Hour, Date, Place.	Summary of Events and Information.	Remarks and references to Appendices.
28 May – 11 June. HERZEELE	During this period the unit J.S. is continuing the Battalion (which had lost from various causes the majority of the Officers and S.C.O's) was proceeded with.	J.S.
12 June. RENINGHELST.	Battalion proceeded to billets in Camp at VOORMEZEELE near DICKEBUSCH	J.S.
13 June. VOORMEZEELE	Major H.S. Cockburn, Yorkshire Regiment joined & assumed command. Lts. R. McMahon Capt. C.L. Ogden & Durham L.I. joined.	J.S. J.S.

Gulab Singh & Sons, Calcutta—No. 22 Army C.—5-8-14—1,07,000.

Army Form C. 2118.

WAR DIARY
or
INTELLIGENCE SUMMARY.
(Erase heading not required.)

Instructions regarding War Diaries and Intelligence Summaries are contained in F. S. Regs., Part II, and the Staff Manual respectively. Title pages will be prepared in manuscript.

Hour, Date, Place.	Summary of Events and Information.	Remarks and references to Appendices.
12 noon June 13th DICKEBUSCH	Major H.M. Goodwyn 1/Devon Regt assumed temporary command of the Battn with Capt: V.B. Ramsden 1/S.W. Borderers Actg Adjutant. Battn in billets Brigade Reserve	
" " 14th "	Lt Ansley 1/Devon Regt attached to Battn for duty - O.C. No.4 Coy	
" " 15th "	Capt. Oglesey & 1/2 volunteers]	" O.C. No.1 Coy
" " 17th "	2/Lt. Forster joined Battn from Artists Rifles No. 1 Coy " O.C. No 1 Coy Mortar Pl[atoon] proceeded to BAILLEUL for M.G. Course	
" " 18th new "	The Battn took over trenches from 1/somerset LI Regt, Hd Quarters and 2 Coys No 3 Coy at GORDON FARM	
" " 9 p.m. "	Major E.L. Roddy arrived from h[ome] leave and took over command of No 3 Coy.	
11.30 p.m 19th "	[illegible] night 19-20 L/Corp.l G[?] Wright + Pte Platt were killed in the trenches	
11. " 26th [?] "	Bugr Ogle & 16th Coy + 3 men arrived Capt Denton arrived & took over command of No 2 Coy	
2 p.m. " 22nd "	2/Lt [Harris] returned from h[ome] leave.	
7 p.m " 23rd "	Hd Quarters proceeded to dug-outs near BRASSERIE	
1.30 a.m. " 24th "	Capt Hasting (since promoted) was killed in the trenches, & buried in Military (Cemetery Cemetery 300* S.W. of GORDON FARM. 2/Lt. Anderson transferred from No 2 Coy Command No. 4 [illegible]	
12 midnight " 26th–27th "	Battn relieved by Monmouth Regt in trenches; Hd. Quarters moved to GORDON FARM Coys in dug-outs in RIDGE WOOD	
10.30 p.m. " 27th "	Battn marched to bivouac in Bde Reserve (H 26 d 2.4). 2/Lt Piercy (No.2) + 2/Lt [?] (No.3) arrived in command of a draft of 81 N.C.Os + men.	
" 28th "	Resting - Drills &c. Content by 28th Divn troops in memory[?]	
" 29th "	Resting - Musketry R. Ly/Battr + 2 A.G. [?] - [illegible] drills &c	
" 30th "	Resting - Drills &c. - Lecture on Gas & its prevention by Capt BARLEY 2nd Army Staff.	

[signature]

28th Div.
84th Bde.

WAR DIARY.

2nd CHESHIRE REGT.

JULY.

1 9 1 5.   Attached:-

           Operation Orders
           ....

WAR DIARY
or
INTELLIGENCE SUMMARY.
(Erase heading not required.)

Army Form C. 2118.

Instructions regarding War Diaries and Intelligence Summaries are contained in F.S. Regs., Part II, and the Staff Manual respectively. Title pages will be prepared in manuscript.

Hour, Date, Place.	Summary of Events and Information.	Remarks and references to Appendices.
June 30 near DICKEBUSCH	Resting - Bulls &c - Reconnaissance by certain Officers. Lecture on gas [not favoured by Capt. Barclay G.S. Army Staff]	
July 1 FR	Resting - Drills & route marches	
2 p.m. " "	2/Lt H.M. Patow arrived on posting to 3 Batt'n, no. 3 Coy	
9 p.m. " "	No 2 Coy. found working party digging communication trench BOIS CARRÉ	
July 2nd " "	- N 2: 3 hours work.	
	Reinforcements. half 1 Batt'n 4, 2 R. 9 trained - Reconnaissance by certain officers	
8.30 p.m. " "	No. 3 & ½ No.4 Coy. working party digging communication trenches VIERSTRAAT to M.I. & N2 to S Redoubt in BOIS CARRÉ.	
	Lt. Newell wounded in attempt at 12 a.m. Killed Habit - engaged in above operation	
	2/Lt Rimmington joined from R.M.C. & posted to No. 1 Coy.	
July 3rd " "	Batt'n worked at DICKEBUSCH HUTS.	
12 Noon 4th	Divine Service at bivouac	
8.30 p.m. " "	Batt'n moved to trenches on left of N3 Rg. of BRASSERIE F'm	
11 p.m. " "	Capt. Lonergan wounded during relief at trench	
10 a.m. 5th -	1 Operation Style. Fell in near vicinity of Batt'n H.Qrs. 1 man slightly wounded - Lt. Newell died of wounds	

Army Form C. 2118.

WAR DIARY
or
INTELLIGENCE SUMMARY.
(Erase heading not required.)

Instructions regarding War Diaries and Intelligence Summaries are contained in F. S. Regs., Part II, and the Staff Manual respectively. Title pages will be prepared in manuscript.

Hour, Date, Place.	Summary of Events and Information.	Remarks and references to Appendices.
9 p.m. 5th July near DICKEBUSCH	Draft of 6 N.C.O.'s & men arrived. Colt. & 1st Aug 2nd R.G. Ramsden proceeded on 5 days privilege leave to England.	
6 p.m. 6th " "	1 man wounded in Trenches	
9 p.m. 7th " "	Some stray hugs fired at support trenches, 3 men wounded. Capt. Freeman joined from S.E.O. as adjutant to 2/Cheshire.	
9 p.m. 8th " "		
9 p.m. 9th " "	Capts. Snow roll & Floyd, 2/Lieut. A. Doney & Walker arrived from England. 2/Lieut. Cole divined from R.E. Course.	
10 p.m. 9th " "	2/Lt. Roseigh accidentally injured by tripping over a rifle in Trenches. Bullet entered left leg - Other casualties 2 men wounded	
10.30 a.m. 10th " "	RIDGEWOOD Shelled for a short time. 2 men of Buffs wounded.	
7 a.m. 11th " "	2 men wounded by shell fire in fire trenches	
12 noon 11th " "	1 man killed by rifle bullet in fire trench	
12 " "	2/Lt. Cole Sent to hospital, asthma. Capt. Ramsden returned from leave.	
5.30 p.m. 12th " "	10 percussion shells fell in & near Battn Hd. Quarters. No casualties	
12.30 p.m. 13th " "	Relief by 3rd R. Fus. Completed and Battn. proceeded to huts at ROSENDAHL BEEK	
2 p.m. 14th " ROSENDAHL BEEK	C.O., Coy Commanders, & M.G. Officer reconnoitred Trenches G.1 - H4 near KEMMEL occupied by 2/East Yorkshire Regt.	

WAR DIARY
or
INTELLIGENCE SUMMARY.
(Erase heading not required.)

Army Form C. 2118.

Hour, Date, Place.	Summary of Events and Information.	Remarks and references to Appendices.
16th Sept		
8 p.m. ROSENDAHL BEEK	Battn marched to billets and bivouacs at WESTOUTRE.	
7 p.m. 15/2 Sept WESTOUTRE	Battn marched to trenches G.1 – H.4 near KEMMEL, relief completed 1.30 a.2. without casualties.	
16th July KEMMEL	Very wet, quiet, no casualties.	
10-30 p.m. " "	1 Coy & 1 M.G. of 6/Welch Reg: attached to Battn in trenches. 2/Lt. Metherell & 34 men rejoined Battn from hutts at POPERINGHE	
17th " "	Very wet – No 3 Coy shelled but no casualties	
18th " "	Fine – No. 3 Coy shelled, 3 casualties, wounded, from rifle fire in evening.	
19th " "	Quiet day, a little shelling. 1 casualty from rifle fire wounded	
20th " "	Battn marched to billets at LOCRE. Very quiet day, finely, cleanly Arrived 3 a.m. 21st relieved in trenches by 1/Suffolks. Battn had but one bath, change of underclothing at new billets	
21st " LOCRE	LOCRE.	
22nd " "	Coy Parades. Had remainder of Battn had baths.	
23rd " "	Coy Parades	
24th " "	Coy Parades	
6-30 p.m. 24th " "	Conduct by 85th Brigade Field Ambulance members, for Battn	

Army Form C. 2118.

WAR DIARY
or
INTELLIGENCE SUMMARY.
(Erase heading not required.)

Instructions regarding War Diaries and Intelligence Summaries are contained in F.S. Regs., Part II, and the Staff Manual respectively. Title pages will be prepared in manuscript.

Hour, Date, Place.	Summary of Events and Information.	Remarks and references to Appendices.
LOERE July 25th	Capt & Adjt A.R. Hill arrived from sick leave from Portland	
11-45 a.m. " 26th "	Butter Parade for divine service near BADAJOS HUTS	
Lecture " 26th "	Batt. moved to trenches G1–H2 rear KEMMEL and took	
1 p.m. 26th "	over from 1/ Suffolks. Relief complete –	
	This period relief not effected	
7.45 p.m. 27th "	Batt. moved to trenches H2 – J3 & rear KEMMEL and took	
	over from 1/ York & Lancs. Regt. Relief completed 11-45	
	p.m. No casualties	
2 a.m. 28th in TRENCHES	1 man slightly wounded	
	Rest of day quiet. 2/Lt. Cameron joined in evening and	
	posted to No. 4 Coy.	
9 a.m. 29th " "	Mine exploded by our mining Coy in trench J32; German	
	infilade Horn in ;	
4 p.m. 29th " "	Henry Philby, Villiers, Brigade HQ function; 1 man 2/ Cheshires	
	wounded at village KEMMEL SCHOOL–	
	2/Lt. Allott transferred to 1/ Cheshire Regt.	
30th " "	Capt Philby or other trenches; Casualties 1 man killed and	
	1 wounded.	
31st " "	Fairly quiet in trenches; Casualties 1 man killed	

OPERATION ORDERS.

Operation Order No. 5 Copy No. 1
by
Major GOODWYN
Commd. 2 Cheshire R/.

27. 7. 14.

1. The Battalion will relieve 1st Y & L. Regt in trenches as under to-night.

2. One Officer per Company will take over trench stores etc. reporting at ROSSIGNOL FARM at 4 p.m.
Each of these Officers will take his Company Hd. Qr. guide who will inspect the exact positions of his Company trenches returning to ROSSIGNOL after.

3. Signal stations will be taken over at 3 p.m. The N.C.O in charge signallers reporting at ROSSIGNOL FARM on arrival.

4. The M.G. Officer will relieve M.Gs in trenches H3. J1. J4 S.P. 12 making his own arrangements for guides. This relief to be effected by 8 p.m.

5. Companies will parade at 7.45 p.m and march independently by Trench parties to DOCTORS HOUSE KEMMEL - where guides will meet the trench parties of 3. 2 & 1 companies. Route via KEMMEL HILL.

③

5. Trench parties to be told off as follows with 100 yards interval which will be maintained throughout.

No 4 Coy { H 4   60.
           H 3   45
           H 2   60

No 3 Coy. { J 1   60
            J 2   45
            J 10   35
            H 5   75 (Remainder of Coy + 1 platoon No 1 Coy)

No 2 Coy. { J 3 R   15
            J 3 new   30
            J 3 L   30
            J * 4   30
            J * 11   50

No 1 Coy   S P 11   ½ platoon.
          S P 12   ½ platoon
Two platoons No 1 Coy will act as Bn Reserve and be billetted at KEMMEL SCHOOL

6. Battalion H^d Qrs ROSSIGNOL FARM

7. Battle H^d Qrs Dug out at H 5

8. Medical Aid Post ROSSIGNOL FARM

3

9. A limber will take 100 full cans of water and hand them over to men in charge of water carts at the Battalion Dump

10. Battalion Reserve will carry them to the trenches and hand over 25 to each Coy on morning of 28th

10. Companies will immediately report by signal message to Bn Hd Qrs completion of relief.

Copy No 1 Record
  - No 2 O.C.
  - No 3 No 1 Coy   R Hunter.
  - No 4 No 2 -
  - No 5 No 3 -   Coy 2/Ches R
  - No 6 No 4 -
  - No 7 M.G.O
     No 8 {Transport} Officer
          {Medical }
          {Quartermaster}
Issued at

Not to be taken into the Trenches   Copy No. 4

OPERATION ORDER No.39
by
Brigadier-General L.J.Bols, C.B.,D.S.O.,
Commanding 84th Infantry Brigade.

Headquarters, 27th July 1915.

Reference
Trench Map 1/10,000.

Reliefs. 1. Reliefs will take place in accordance with the attached Table A. The portion of 1st Welch Regiment relieved on night of 27th/28th will leave the trenches via Regent Street.

March. 2. The 2nd Cheshire Regt. will be clear of the barrier on the LOCRE Road by 8.45 p.m. The 2nd Northd.Fusiliers will not pass the barrier before 8.45 p.m.

Billets. 3. Battalions on relief will be disposed as shown in attached Table B.

Machine-Guns. 4. Machine-Guns will be relieved and disposed as follows, on 27th inst.

Unit taking over.	Emplacement.	Unit handing over.
2nd Northd.Fusiliers.	F.5	1st Welch Regiment.
---do---	G.1,G.3,G.4a	1st Suffolk Regiment.
2nd Cheshire Regt.	H.3	1st Suffolk Regiment.
---do---	J.1,J.4,S.P.12	Y & L Rgt.83rd Bde.
6th Welch Regt.	S.P.10	2nd Northd.Fusiliers.
---do---	S.P.11	6th Welch Regt.
Monmouth Regt.	S.P.8,S.P.9	2nd Northd.Fusiliers.

On 28th inst..
| Monmouth Regt. | F.2, F.4. | 1st Welch Regt. |
| E.Surrey,85thBde. | E.2 | 1st Welch Regt. |

The above reliefs of Machine guns and their detachments will be effected before 8 p.m. on the date mentioned.
Guns in the fire trenches are not to leave until the respective reliefs have arrived.
~~Guns in the fire trenches~~ Machine Gun officers of units taking over will arrange direct with those of units handing over as to time and method of relief and for guides as required.

Reconnaissance. 5. All necessary reconnaissance to be carried out before taking over.

Trench Stores. 6. All trench stores to be handed over and receipts given and obtained respectively. Copies of these receipts will be rendered to Bde.H.Q. by 11 a.m. 30th inst. Any shortage or deficiency of stores will be reported immediately to Bde. Headquarters.

Command. 7. Commanding Officers of Units handing over will remain in Command until the relief of their respective Battalions has been completed.

Headqrs. 8. Battn.H.Q. will be established as follows:-
Right Sector CHALET N 27 c 2.9
Centre Sector DOCTOR'S HOUSE N 21 d 8.4
Left Sector ROSSIGNOL N 22 a 3.4

Reports. 9. *See over*

Reports. 9. Completion of reliefs will be reported by wire to Brigade Headquarters immediately they are effected.

R Q Crawfurd

Issued at ...11. a.m.....

Captain,
Brigade Major,
84th Infantry Bde.

```
Copy No.1   Retained.
 "   No.2   2nd Northd.Fusiliers.
 "   No.3.  1st Suffolk Regiment.
 "   No.4   2nd Cheshire Regiment.
 "   No.5   1st Welch Regiment.
 "   No.6   Monmouth Regiment.
 "   No.7   6th Welch Regiment.
 "   No.8   31st Brigade, R.F.A.
 "   No.9   83rd Infantry Bde.
 "   No.10  85th Infantry Bde.
```

TABLE "A".

Unit taking over.	Trench number	GARRISON				Unit handing over.	date of relief.
		Fire trench	Suppt trch.	S.P.	Res.		
85th Brigade.	E.2	70M.G.	-	-	-	1st Welch	28/29
xxxxxxxxxxxxx	F.6	-	30	-	-	-do-	28/29
Monmouth Regt.	F.2	65M.G.				-do-	28/29
	F.6		40			-do-	"
	*F.4	70M.G.				-do-	"
	F.6		40			-do-	"
	S.P.8			25MG		6th Welch	"
	S.P.9			30MG		-do-	"
	R.S.D.O.				60	1st Welch	"
		135	80	55	60	Total 330 & 4 M.Gs
2nd Northd.Fus.	F.5	70M.G.				1st Welch	27/28
"	F.6		40			-do-	"
"	G.1	65M.G.				1st Suffolk	"
"	G.2	85				-do-	"
"	Suppts		80			-do-	"
"	G.3	80M.G.				-do-	"
"	G.4a	55M.G.				-do-	"
"	G.4		50			-do-	"
"	New sap	65				-do-	"
"	H.1		55			-do-	"
"	S.P.10			25MG		6th Welch	"
"	%Reserve				60	1st Suffolk	"
		420	225	25	60	Total 730 & 5 M.Gs.
nd Ches:Regt.	H.2	60				1st Suffolk	27/28
"	H.3	45M.G.				-do-	"
"	H.4	60				-do-	"
"	J.1	60M.G.				Y & L Regt.	"
"	J.2	45				-do-	"
"	J.10		35			-do-	"
"	H.5		75			-do-	"
"	J.3R	15				-do-	"
"	J.3new	30				-do-	"
"	J.3L	30				-do-	"
"	J.11		50			-do-	"
"	J.4		30MG			-do-	"
	S.P.11			30MG		6th Welch	"
	S.P.12			30MG		Y & L Regt	"
	%Reserve				60	Suffolk Rgt	"
		345	190	60	60	Total 655 & 5 M.Gs.

New junction between F.4 & F.5 as marked in trench.
n Kemmel School.

TABLE "B".

Date.	Right Sector.	Centre Sector.	Left Sector.	Locre. (Monmouth Shelters.	Kemmel	Arcadia.
27/28	1st Welch	2nd N.Fuslrs.	2nd Ches.R.	1st Suff. nil		6th Welch
28/29	Mon.Regt.	2nd N.Fuslrs.	2nd Ches.R.	1st Suff. nil / WELCH		6th Welch

28th Div.
84th Bde.

WAR DIARY.

2nd CHESHIRE REGT.

A U G U S T

1 9 1 5.

Attached:-
Operation Orders.

Army Form C. 2118.

WAR DIARY
or
INTELLIGENCE SUMMARY.
(Erase heading not required.)

Instructions regarding War Diaries and Intelligence Summaries are contained in F. S. Regs., Part II, and the Staff Manual respectively. Title pages will be prepared in manuscript.

Hour, Date, Place.	Summary of Events and Information.	Remarks and references to Appendices.
Aug 1 Trenches near KEMMEL	Quiet day in trenches 1 man accidentally wounded	RM
9 a.m. 2nd - -	About 30 shells fired at Battery near Bn Hd Qrs without damage Quiet in trenches - no casualties	RM
3rd - -	Some shelling & trench mortars used on left of our trenches 1 man slightly wounded 1 rifle bullet.	
3rd - -	Enemy exploded mine in G Trenches occupied 1 Welch R.	
1 a.m 4th - -	Bn relieved 1 YORK & LANCASTER R and marches to billets in LOCRE.	RM
5. p.m. 6 LOCRE	Lieut Col T. H. F PEARSE C.M.G. returned from sick leave and resumed command of Bn.	RM
3.45 p.m. 7 KEMMEL -	A draft of 20 men arrived for the Bn.	RM
8.0 p.m 7 KEMMEL SHELTERS	The Bn moved to KEMMEL SHELTERS relieving Monmouth R.	B. O. O. 41. & 8 Cwi.
8.0 p.m 8 -	230 men employed on Bde working party.	RM
8.0 p m 9 -	300 men employed on Bde working party	RM

Army Form C. 2118.

WAR DIARY
or
INTELLIGENCE SUMMARY.
(Erase heading not required.)

Instructions regarding War Diaries and Intelligence Summaries are contained in F. S. Regs., Part II, and the Staff Manual respectively. Title pages will be prepared in manuscript.

Hour, Date, Place.	Summary of Events and Information.	Remarks and references to Appendices.
3.30 p.m. 11. KEMMEL	Lieut ELKINGTON RAMC. arrived to relieve Lieut BROWN RAMC	
7.15 p.m. 11. KEMMEL SHELTERS.	The Bn. moved out to relieve 1 SUFFOLK R. in trenches on Kemmel.	B.O.O. 42 of 10 Aug.
	The trenches. 1 Company 7 Leicester Reg. attached to the Bn. for instruction.	R.O.O. 10 of 11 Aug.
12 noon 11-12 Aug. near LINDENHOEK	Relief completed.	
12 Trenches near LINDENHOEK.	Enemy exploded a mine in front of one of trenches held by No 1 Coy. with apparent intention of demolishing house. No	
5 A.m. 12 inst.	damage to trenches.	
4. p.m. "	O.C. no 2 reports loopholes area curious construction in front German redoubt similar to those used for use of liquid fire.	2A
5 p.m. "	Trench opposite redoubt cleared whilst Howitzer battery shelled German redoubt. No apparent damage.	
12 noon 13-14 "	Platoons 7 Leicester Reg. attached to Coys. returned, and B Coy 2/4 7 Leicester Reg took over trenches of No 1 Co.	3M
	Lt. PICKARD left for HELFAUT.	
9.30 p.m. 15 Aug.	A draft of 105 men arrived for the Battalion. Major GOODWYN left to rejoin 1. DEVON R.	RM
8 a.m. 16 Aug.	Loophole in front of 14a trenches shelled by one howitzer. No apparent damage.	RM

Army Form C. 2118.

WAR DIARY
or
INTELLIGENCE SUMMARY.
(Erase heading not required.)

Instructions regarding War Diaries and Intelligence Summaries are contained in F.S. Regs., Part II, and the Staff Manual respectively. Title pages will be prepared in manuscript.

Hour, Date, Place.	Summary of Events and Information.	Remarks and references to Appendices.
5 P.M. Aug 16 Trenches nr LINDENHOEK	Hostile batteries again bombarded our trenches which was damaged to a certain extent.	P.M.
8.0 a.m. Aug 17 " "	No 2 & 4 companies bombarded with rifle grenades 16 casualties	
10 a.m. " " "	Enemy shell communication trench in rear of J.15 return.	P.M.
Aug. 19 LOTRE	The Bn was relieved by 1st SUFFOLK REGT	B.O.O. 44 } R.O.O. 13. }
Aug. 25 LOTRE	The Bn relieved 1st SUFFOLK REGT in the trenches, and	B.O.O. 49. R.M
29/30 Aug.	Bn on relief { 1st SUFFOLK REGT proceeded to BADAJOS HUTS	B.O.O. 49 R.O.O. 14. }
	LOTRE	
12.20 A.M. 30 Aug LOTRE.	Bn arrived LOTRE	
3.30 P.M. " "	Bn inspected by G.O.C. 2nd ARMY	
6 P.M. "	Bn found working parties of 450 men for trenching at KEMMEL	R.M.
3130 p.m. 31 Aug —	Bn moved to KEMMEL SHELTERS.	R.O.D. 15.
		P.M.

Unsworthy Major Comndg.
2 B". Cheshire R.
2.9.15

OPERATION

ORDERS.

Copy No. 4

OPERATION ORDER No. 40
by
Brigadier-General L.J.Bols, C.B., D.S.O.,
Commanding 84th Infantry Brigade.

Secret

Not to be taken to trenches

Headquarters, 2nd August 1915.

Reliefs. 1. On the night of 2nd/3rd August the 1st Welch Regiment and 6th Welch Regiment (less 1 company) will take over trenches as per attached table.

On night of 3rd/4th August a battalion of 83rd Brigade will take over trenches now held by 2nd Cheshire Regiment, with the exception of S.P.11, which will be taken over by 1st Welch Regiment on night of 2nd/3rd August.

On the night of 4th/5th August, 1st Suffolk Regt. will take over trenches from 85th Brigade as per attached table.

Machine Guns. 2. Machine guns will be located and manned as follows:-

(a) Machine guns in G.4a, G.3, G.1 now found by 2nd Northumberland Fusiliers, and in S.P.11 now found by 6th Welch Regiment, will be relieved by 1st Welch Regiment.

(b) Machine gun in F.5 now found by 2nd Northd.Fusiliers will remain there.

(c) Machine gun in S.P.10 now found by 6th Welch Regiment will be relieved by a gun and detachment of 2nd Northd.Fusiliers to proceed there on relief by 1st Welch Regiment.

(d) The machine guns in F.4 and F.2 now found by Monmouth Regt: will be relieved by the 6th Welch Regiment to proceed there on relief by 2nd Northd.Fusiliers and 1st Welch Regt. respectively.

(e) The Machine guns in S.P.8 and 9 now found by Monmouth Regt: will remain there, the 6th Welch Regiment providing the detachments for these guns.

(f) O.C.Units whose guns remain in action will arrange to provide frest detachments for same except where otherwise stated.

(g)

2.

    (g) All above reliefs to take place before 8 p.m. 2nd August. No machine gun to be withdrawn from the front trench before being relieved.

    (h) Machine guns in E.2, L.15 and S.P.7 now found by 85th Brigade, will be relieved by 1st Suffolk Regiment at same time as relief of battalion is effected.

Billets. 3.   Battalions will be accommodated as follows:-

On relief, 2nd Northd. Fusiliers will proceed to billets in LOCRE vacated by 1st Welch Regiment.

On relief, Monmouth Regiment will proceed to billets in LOCRE vacated by 6th Welch Regiment - 1 company of 6th Welch Regiment remaining in these billets with Monmouth Regiment.

On relief, 2nd Cheshire Regiment will proceed to billets in LOCRE vacated by the battalion of 83rd Brigade.

On night of 4th/5th the Monmouth Regiment and 1 company 6th Welch Regiment, which will be attached to Monmouth Regt for tactical purposes only, will move into KEMMEL shelters vacated by 1st Suffolk Regiment, and the 2nd Cheshire Regt will take over the billets vacated by Monmouth Regiment and attached company 6th Welch Regiment.

Head Quarters 4.   Head Quarters of Battalions in front line will be established as follows:-

    Left Battalion ... DOCTOR'S HOUSE.
    Centre Battalion ... CHALET LINDENHOEK.
    Right Battalion. ... TEA FARM N 34 D 1.7

Stores. 5.   All trench stores will be handed over to incoming battalions and a receipt obtained. A copy of receipt for stores in trenches taken over by 1st Suffolk Regiment will be rendered to Brigade Headquarters before 11 a.m. 6th inst.

Receipts. 6.   Officers Commanding units handing over will remain in command of line until relief is completed. The fact of the OcC. incoming unit having taken over command will be notified in the report of completion of relief.

Reconnaissance.

3.

Reconnaissance.

    7.   All necessary reconnaissance will be carried out before taking over.

Guides. 8.   Officers Commanding Battalions concerned will arrange direct as to method of relief and guides.

Reports. 9.   Completion of all reliefs will be reported to Brigade Headquarters by wire as soon as effected.

R.D. Crawfurd.

Issued at .....8am.......

Captain,
Brigade Major,
84th Infantry Brigade.

Copy No.1 Retained.
" " 2 2nd Northd. Fusiliers.
" " 3 1st Suffolk Regiment.
" " 4 2nd Cheshire Regiment.
" " 5 1st Welch Regiment.
" " 6 Monmouth Regiment.
" " 7 6th Welch Regiment.
" " 8 31st Brigade R.F.A.
" " 9 No.3 Company, A.S.C.
" " 10 83rd Infantry Bde.
" " 11 85th Infantry Bde.
" " 12

Unit taking over	Trench number	Fire trench	Support trench	S.P.	Res.	Unit handing over.	date.
1st Welch Regt.	S.P. 11			30MG		2nd Ches.R.	2/3rd
	S.P.10			25MG		2nd N.Fuslrs.	"
	H.1		55			"	"
	new sap.	65				"	"
	G.4		50			"	"
	G.4a	55MG				"	"
	G.3	80MG				"	"
	G.2	85				"	"
	G.1	65MG			*	"	"
	Supports		80		140		
		350	185	55	140	Total 730 & 5 M.Gs.	
6th Welch Regt. less 1 company.	F.5	70MG				2nd N.Fuslrs.	2/3rd.
	F.6		40			"	"
	F.4	70MG				Monmouth R.	"
	F.6		80			"	"
x	F.2	65MG				"	"
	F.6		40			"	"
	S.P.8			25MG		"	"
	S.P.9			30MG		"	"
	R.S.D.O.				100	"	"
		205	160	55	100	Total 520 & 5 M.Gs	
1st Suffolk R.	E.2	70MG				Battalion of 4/5th 85th Bde.	
	E.1	80				"	"
	E.3		40			"	"
	E.4		50			"	"
	E.6		70			"	"
	S.P.7			25MG		"	"
15	L.6	150 & 2MGs				"	"
15 S	L.6s	40	40			"	"
14 a r b	L.4	110				"	"
14 S	L.4s		40			"	"
	Pond) Farm)				120	"	"
		450	200	25	120	Total 795 & 4 M.Gs	

* Kemmel School.

OPERATION ORDER No.41.   Copy No. 8

by
Brigadier-General L.J.Bols, C.B., D.S.O.,
Commanding 84th Infantry Brigade.
Headquarters, 8th August 1915.

1. Reliefs.
On night of 9th/10th inst: the 2nd Northd: Fusiliers with one company 7th Leicester Regt: will take over the trenches now held by 1st Welch Regt:, and in addition will take over trenches F.5 70 and F.4 70 and supports to same in P.6 80 from 6th Welch Regt:.

On same night the company 6th Welch Regt:. now with Monmouth Regt: will take over REGENT STREET Dug-outs and come under the command of O.C. 2nd N.Fusrs: for all tactical and working purposes.

On 9th inst: one company 7th Leicester Regt: will be attached to 1st Suffolk Regt: and 1st Suffolk Regt: will take over F.2 70 support to same in F.6 40, S.P.8 25 and S.P.9 50. The company of 7th Leicester Regt: to be ready to move at 4 p.m. under instructions from O.C.1st Suffolk Regiment.

2. Attachment.
The companies of 7th Leicester Regiment will be utilised in the fire and support trenches and will be distributed by platoons throughout the line, each officer, N.C.O. and man going on duty with his opposite number. They will not be employed individually.

3. Rations.
The O.C.6th Welch Regiment will arrange to ration the company in REGENT STREET Dugouts. The arrangements for rations for the two companies 7th Leicester Regiment will be made direct between the Commanding Officers concerned.

4. Machine Guns.
Machine Guns will be redistributed on 9th inst: as follows:-

2nd N.Fusiliers will relieve 1st Welch machine guns in G.1 G.3 and G.4a.

2.

1st Welch Regiment machine guns from G.1 will proceed to S.P.10 on relief by 2nd N.Fusiliers.

6th Welch Regiment machine Guns will remain in F.2 and F.4.

1st Monmouth Regiment will provide a detachment without guns for S.P.8 and S.P.9.

The 2nd N.Fusilier gun from S.P.10 will relieve the 1st Welch Regiment Gun in G.1 by 6 p.m.

All other machine gun reliefs will be completed by 8.p.m.

5. Trench Stores. All trench stores will be handed over and receipts given and obtained respectively.

6. Billets. The 1st Welch Regiment on relief will occupy the billets vacated by 2nd N.Fusiliers. The 6th Welch Regt: will be notified later as to where they will be billeted onrelief tomorrow night.

7. Training. The attention of all concerned is drawn to the programmeof training attached.

The companies of the 7th Leicester Regt: are to be instructed in all the details and methods of trench warfare and in the method of rationing and reliefs etc.

8. Reports. All reliefs and redistribution will be reported to Bde: Headquarters by wire immediately on completion.

Captain,
Brigade Major,
84th Infantry Bde.

Issued at 5.15 p.m.

No.1 Retained.
No.2 2nd N.Fusiliers.
No.3 1st Suffolk Regt:
No.4 1st Welch Regt.
No.5 Monmouth Regt:
No.6 6th Welch Regt:
No.7 7th Leicester Regt.
No.8 2nd Cheshire Regt. ✓
No.9 110th Infantry Bde.
No.10 31st Brigade R.F.A.

28th Division.

Training of 37th Division in trench warfare.

※※※

The following are the lines on which the training of the units of the 37th Division will be carried out. Details are left to the Brigadiers, who will issue the necessary instructions to their subordinate commanders:-

Infantry.

1st & 2nd days.   Two companies per battalion, 110th Infantry Bde, will be attached to the battalions in the trenches, and will work by platoons under platoon commanders. The remaining two companies per battalion, 110th Infantry Bde: will be attached to battalions in rest billets, and will work similarly by platoons under platoon commanders.

3rd & 4th days.   The companies will continue working by platoons, those in the trenches going into rest billets and those in rest billets going into the trenches.

5th day.   Two companies per battalion will move from rest billets into the trenches and will remain there for 24 hours, and work by companies. Two companies from trenches will move to rest billets for 24 hours and work by companies.

6th day.   The companies in rest billets will relieve the companies in the trenches. Work continued by coys.

7th & 8th days.   The battalions will occupy a section of the front and work by battalions.

Battalions will not be employed in digging, beyond what is considered necessary for their instruction.

For instructional purposes battalions will move camp/once during their period of attachment.

※※※※※※※※※

OPERATION ORDER No.42   Copy No. 4
by
~~Secret~~
Brigadier-General L.J.Bols, C.B., D.S.O.,
Commanding 84th Infantry Brigade.

Not to be taken into trenches.

Headquarters,   10th August 1915.

1. **Reliefs.**   Tomorrow night, 11th/12th August the 2nd Cheshire Regiment with one company 7th Leicester Regiment will take over trenches as below from 1st Suffolk Regiment.

E.2 70 & M.G.	E.3 40	15s 40
E.1 80	E.4 50	14s 40
15 150 & 2 M.Gs.	E.6 70	Newport dugouts 120
14a) 14) 110.	S.P.7 25 & M.G.	

Head Quarters TEA FARM N 34 d 1.7

On same night 1st Monmouth Regiment will take over trenches as below from 1st Suffolk Regiment:

F.2 80 & 1 M.G.	S.P.8 25 & 1 M.G.
F.6 30	S.P.9 30 & 1 M.G.

Head Quarters LINDENHOEK CHALET.

2. **Attachment.**   The company of 7th Leicester Regt: now attached to 2nd Northd:Fusiliers will be relieved by another Company 7th Leicester Regt: tomorrow night 11th/12th August. O.Cs to make arrangements as to method of relief.

The company of 7th Leicester Regiment attached to 2nd Cheshire Regt: will go into the trenches at same time as 2nd Cheshire Regt. O.Cs to arrange direct as to place for rendezvous.

The two companies 7th Leicester Regt: coming out of the trenches will return to their bivouac and be attached for instruction to 1st Welch Regt: who will instruct them in the same manner as the two previous companies.

3. **Reconnaissance.**

9. REGENT STREET DUGOUTS. The company of 6th Welch Regiment now in REGENT STREET DUGOUTS will come under the orders of Officer Commanding 1st Monmouth Regiment for tactical and working purposes on completion of relief of trenches to be taken over by 1st Monmouth Regiment.

3.	Reconnaissance.	All necessary reconnaissance by officer of 2nd Cheshire Regiment to be carried out by day before going into the trenches.
4.	Guides.	Officers Commanding 2nd Cheshire Regt: and 1st Monmouth Regt: will arrange direct with O.C.1st Suffolk Regt: as to method of relief and guides.
5.	Machine-guns.	Machine guns will be relieved as follows:- The 4 machine guns of 2nd Cheshire Regt: will relieve the machine guns of 1st Suffolk Regt: in E.2, two guns in No.15 trench and one in S.P.7. A machine gun of 1st Monmouth Regt: will relieve a machine gun of 6th Welch Regiment in F.2. The remaining machine gun of 1st Monmouth Regt: to be retained at Head Quarters. All other machine guns to remain as at present. Reliefs as ordered to be completed before 8 p.m.
6.	Bivouacs.	On relief the 1st Suffolk Regiment will proceed to KEMMEL SHELTERS and take over bivouacs and shelters vacated by 2nd Cheshire Regiment.
7.	Trench stores.	All trench stores to be handed over on relief and receipts given and obtained respectively.
8.	Reports.	Completion of all reliefs to be reported to Brigade Head Quarters by wire as soon as effected.
9.	REGENT STREET DUGOUTS.	The company of 6th Welch Regiment now in REGENT STREET DUGOUTS will come under the orders of Officer Commanding 1st Monmouth Regiment for tactical and working purposes on completion of relief of trenches to be taken over by 1st Monmouth Regiment.

```
Copy No.3  1st Suffolk Regiment.
Copy No.4  2nd Cheshire Regiment.
Copy No.5  1st Welch Regiment.
Copy No.6  Monmouth Regiment.
Copy No.7  6th Welch Regiment.
Copy No.8  7th Leicester Regiment.
Copy No.9  110th Infantry Brigade.
Copy No10  31st Brigade, R.F.A.
Copy No11  No.3 Company, A.S.C.
```

3. Reconnaissance. All necessary reconnaissance by officer of 2nd Cheshire Regiment to be carried out by day before going into the trenches.

4. Guides. Officers Commanding 2nd Cheshire Regt: and 1st Monmouth Regt: will arrange direct with O.C.1st Suffolk Regt: as to method of relief and guides.

5. Machine-guns. Machine guns will be relieved as follows:-

The 4 machine guns of 2nd Cheshire Regt: will relieve the machine guns of 1st Suffolk Regt: in E.2, two guns in No.15 trench and one in S.P.7.

A machine gun of 1st Monmouth Regt: will relieve a machine gun of 6th Welch Regiment in F.2.

The remaining machine gun of 1st Monmouth Regt: to be retained at Head Quarters.

All other machine guns to remain as at present.

Reliefs as ordered to be completed before 8 p.m.

6. Bivouacs. On relief the 1st Suffolk Regiment will proceed to KEMMEL SHELTERS and take over bivouacs and shelters vacated by 2nd Cheshire Regiment.

7. Trench stores. All trench stores to be handed over on relief and receipts given and obtained respectively.

8. Reports. Completion of all reliefs to be reported to Brigade Head Quarters by wire as soon as effected.

Issued at 7.pm.

R.D. Crawfurd.
Captain,
Brigade Major,
84th Infantry Bde.

Copy No.1 retained.
Copy No.2 2nd Northd:Fusiliers.
Copy No.3 1st Suffolk Regiment.
Copy No.4 2nd Cheshire Regiment.
Copy No.5 1st Welch Regiment.
Copy No.6 Monmouth Regiment.
Copy No.7 6th Welch Regiment.
Copy No.8 7th Leicester Regiment.
Copy No.9 110th Infantry Brigade.
Copy No10 31st Brigade, R.F.A.
Copy No11 No.3 Company, A.S.C.

OPERATION ORDER No.43   Copy No. 4
                    by   Secret
        Brigadier-General L.J.Bols, C.B., D.S.O.,
              Commanding 84th Infantry Brigade.

Not to be taken to the trenches

                    Headquarters 14th August 1915.

Reliefs.   1. On the night of the 15th/16th August the ~~7th Bn Leicester~~ 6 Welch
                Regiment will take over trenches as below and hold this
                front as a complete battalion. The two companies 7th
                Leicester Regt now in the trenches will come under the
                command of O.C.7th Leicester Regt on completion of releif
                of the remaining trenches.

            2. Trench   Fire   Support Supptg   Reserve Unit handing over
                number   trench trench   point

                E.3   40   Now held by 7th
                                                             Leicester Regt.
                E.6   70   --do--
                E.2   70 & MG   --do--
                F.2   80 & MG   1st Monmouth R.
                Support to   40   --do--
                F.2 in F.6
                F.4   70 & MG   Now held by 7th
                                                             Leicester Regt.
                Support to   40   --do--
                F.4 in F.6
                F.5   70 & MG   2nd N.Fusiliers.
                Support to   40   Now held by 7th
                F.5 in F.6   Leicester Regt.
                S.P.8   25 & MG   1st Monmouth R.
                S.P.9   30 & MG   --do--
                S.P.10   25 & MG   Now held by 7th
                                                             Leicester Regt.
                Regent St.   120   6th Welch Regt.
                Dug-outs.
                         _____
                         360   160   80   120   Total 720 & 7 MGs.

                Headquarters 7th Leicester Regt will be at LINDENHOEK
                CHALET N 27 c 3.9

Machine guns. 3. Machine guns as provided at present will remain in the
                trenches, the M.G.Detachment of 7th Leicester Regiment
                being attached to them for instruction under arrangements
                to be made by O.C.7th Leicester Regiment.

Trench stores. 4. All trench stores will be handed over and receipts given

given and obtained respectively. The O.C.7th Leicester Regt will arrange to take over the stores not already held by the companies of his battalion, by daylight 15th inst.

Reconnaissance. 5. Company Officers taking over new trenches or effecting any redistribution will carry out a reconnaissance of the trenches by daylight before 12 noon 15th inst.

Method of relief. 6. O.C.7th Leicester Regt will arrange direct with O.C.2nd N. Fusiliers and O.C.1st Monmouth Regt as to method of relief.

Conference Cancelled 7. The Officer Commanding, 2nd in Command, Adjutant and Quartermaster of 7th Leicester Regt will assemble at 84th Brigade Headquarters at 2.30 p.m. today 14th August, to discuss details and arrange for taking over.

Command 8. The O.C.7th Leicester Regt will assume command of the line held by his battalion as soon as the completion of the relief of those portions of the line held by 1st Monmouth Regt and 2nd Northd Fusiliers is completed.

Report 9. The completion of the relief and the time at which the O.C. 7th Leicester Regt assumes command will be reported by wire to 84th Brigade Headquarters as soon as effected.

R.D. Crawford
Captain,
Brigade Major,
84th Infantry Brigade.

14th August 1915.

Issued at 8.30 a.m.

No.1 Retained.
No.2 2nd Northd.Fusiliers.
No.3 1st Suffolk Regt.
No.4 2nd Cheshire Regt.
No.5 1st Welch Regt.
No.6 1st Monmouth Regt.
No.7 6th Welch Regy.
No.8 7th Leicester Regt.
No.9 110th Infantry Bde.
No.10 31st Brigade R.F.A.
No.11 No.3 Coy.A.S.C.

OPERATION ORDER No.44   Copy No. 4

by

Brigadier-General L.J.Bols, C.B., D.S.O.,

Commanding 84th Infantry Brigade.

Secret

Not to be taken to the trenches.

17th August 1915.

1. On the night of 18th/19th August the 1st Suffolk Regiment will take over the trenches now held by the 2nd Cheshire Regiment, and in addition E.3 (garrison 40 men) now held by the 6th Welch Regiment.

2. Machine guns of the 2nd Cheshire Regiment will be relieved by the machine guns of 1st Suffolk Regiment by 8 p.m. 18th August.

3. Officers Commanding 2nd Cheshire Regiment and 6th Welch Regiment will remain in command until reliefs are completed.

4. On relief 2nd Cheshire Regiment will move to BADAJOS HUTS.

E. Gepp.

Major,
Brigade Major,
84th Infantry Brigade.

Issued at ....

Copy No.1 Retained.
Copy No.2 2nd Northd:Fusiliers.
Copy No.3 1st Suffolk Regiment.
Copy No.4 2nd Cheshire Regiment.
Copy No.5 1st Welch Regiment.
Copy No.6 1st Monmouth Regiment.
Copy No.7 6th Welch Regiment.
Copy No.8 31st Brigade, R.F.A.
Copy No.9 No.3 Company, A.S.C.

OPERATION ORDER No.46   Copy No. 4
by
Brigadier-General L.J.Bols, C.B., D.S.O.,   Secret
Commanding 84th Infantry Brigade.

Not to be taken into the trenches

21st August 1915.

1. On the night 22nd/23rd August Officer Commanding 6th Welch Regiment will relieve his two companies in the trenches, except that S.P.8 (1 officer, 25 men) and S.P.9 (1 officer, 30 men) will be relieved the same night by 1st Monmouth Regiment.

2. The 1st Monmouth Regiment will also relieve the Machine Guns in S.P.8 and S.P.9, reliefs to be completed by 8 p.m.

E.C. Gepp
Major,
Brigade Major,
84th Infantry Brigade.

Issued at 10-30 a.m.

No.1 Retained.
No.2 2nd Northd:Fusiliers.
No.3 1st Suffolk Regiment.
No.4 2nd Cheshire Regiment.
No.5 1st Welch Regiment.
No.6 1st Monmouth Regiment.
No.7 6th Welch Regiment.

OPERATION ORDER No.47   Copy No. 4

by

Brigadier-General L.J.Bols, C.B., D.S.O.,
Commanding 84th Infantry Brigade.

Secret
*Not to be taken
into the trenches*

23rd August 1915.

1.   (a) On night 24th/25th August 2nd Northd:Fusiliers will relieve 1st Welch Regiment.

    (b) On 24th August 2nd Northd:Fusiliers will relieve machine gunners of 1st Welch Regiment in F.5, G.1, G.3 & S.P.10. Reliefs to be completed by 8 p.m.

    (c) On relief 1st Welch will move to Kemmel Shelters.

2.   (a) On night 25th/26th August 2nd Cheshire Regiment will relieve 1st Suffolk Regiment.

    (b) On 25th August 2nd Cheshire Regiment will relieve machine gunners of 1st Suffolk Regiment in 15 (2 guns), E.2 & S.P.7. Relief to be completed by 8 p.m.

    (c) On relief 1st Suffolk Regiment will move to BADAJOS Huts.

3.   Officers Commanding 1st Welch Regiment and 1st Suffolk Regiment will command until relief of their trenches is completed.

E.C. Gepp.
Major,
Brigade Major,
84th Infantry Brigade.

Issued at 2.15 p.m.

No.1 Retained.
No.2 2nd Northd:Fusiliers.
No.3 1st Suffolk Regt.
No.4 2nd Cheshire Regt.
No.5 1st Welch Regiment.
No.6 1st Monmouth Regt.
No.7 6th Welch Regt.
No.8 31st Brigade, R.F.A.
No.9 85th Infantry Bde.
No10 83rd Infantry Bde.
No11 No.3 Company, A.S.C.

File with Operation Orders

OPERATION ORDER No.49   Copy No. 4

by

Lieut:Colonel T.H.Finch-Pearse, C.M.G.,

Commanding 84th Infantry Brigade.

28th August 1915.

Secret
Not to be taken
into the trenches

1.   On the night of 29th/30th August 1st Suffolk Regiment will relieve 2nd Cheshire Regiment and their machine guns.

2.   On the night of 30th/31st August 1st Welch Regiment will relieve 2nd Northumberland Fusiliers and their machine guns.

E.C. Gepp.
Major,
Brigade Major,
84th Infantry Brigade.

Issued at 12-35 p.m.

No.1 Retained.
No.2 2nd Northd:Fusiliers.
No.3 1st Suffolk Regt.
No.4 2nd Cheshire Regt.
No.5 1st Welsh Regt.
No.6 1st Monmouth Regt.
No.7 6th Welch Regt.
No.8 31st Brigade, R.F.A.
No.9 Supply Officer, 84th Bde.

Operation Order No. 11   Copy No 1
by
Major GOODWYN Comm'd
2 B'n Cheshire R't
3-8-14

1. The Battalion will be relieved by 1: YORK
& LANCASTER REGT about 9 pm to-night.

2. O.C. Coys will have all trench stores & S.A.A.
checked & ready for handing over this
afternoon.
Receipts to be obtained from the incoming
Company & copies of the same to be
handed to the Adjutant by 12 noon
4 Aug.

3. All small periscopes & water cans to be taken
away on Company charge. The latter to be
carefully packed on a limber which will
be on the road close to Batt'n Dump
BURNT FARM.

4. Guides will be ~~mounted~~ detailed as ~~under~~.
They will report at Bn Hd Qrs at 7.45 pm
from which point they will be marched
in a body to KEMMEL - LA CLYTTE
and report to units taking over

4. Two guides will be detailed from each Company and one from trench H.3 & S.P.12 to report to Battⁿ Hd Qrs at 7.30 P.M. From this point they will be marched in a body to barrier on KEMMEL-LA CLYTTE ROAD & report to Officers in charge of trench parties of units taking over as under:

		Unit taking over	
H.3	M.G.	5ᵗʰ King's Own	} 8.15 p.m.
X S.P.12	M.G.	5ᵗʰ King's Own	
J.3 new.		1ˢᵗ York & Lanc. R.	
J.3 Right.		" " " "	
J.2 Left		" " " "	
J.4		" " " "	
J.#		" " " "	} 8.30 p.m
S.P.12 ?		" " " "	
H.3		5/ King's Own Rgt	
H.3.1		" " " "	
H.4		" " " "	
H.5		" " " "	

5. O.C. Coys will report personally at Bn Hd Qrs on completion of relief & will then march their Companies back to LOCRE

Copy n°

Operation Order no 10
by
Lt. Col. T. H. F. Heath C.M.G.
Comm¹ 2 Bn Cheshire Regt

Ref. map 28.   11. 8. 15

The Batt⁰ will relieve 1ˢᵗ Suffolk Regt in the
trenches to-night

Company Commanders, M.G. Officer, Bombing
Officer, an Officer 7ᵗʰ Leicester Reg., Company
Sergt Majors, Pioneer Sergt and C.O. orderly will
leave Bn. HdQrs KEMMEL shelters at 3 p.m.
to take over trenches.

Signallers will be relieved 5 p.m.
Guards will be relieved 3 p.m
Machine guns will be relieved before 8 p.m.

The Bn will pass starting point (Bn. HdQrs
KEMMEL shelters) as under, and march
via ARCADIA DUG OUTS – LINDENHOEK
cross Roads to junction of roads near BUS
Fm. (N 33 d 4.3) where guides will meet the Bn.
  Company guides and Bombers parade with
Companies.
  Company guides return to Bn Hd Qrs T6 A Fm.
after proceeding to trenches with their Company.

No 2 Coy less 1 platoon + 1 platoon Leicester R. start 7.15 p.m.
  – 4 –   – 1 – + 1 –   –   – 7.20 p.m
  – 3 –   – 1 – + 1 –   –   – 7.25 p.m
  – 1 –   – 1 – + 1 –   –   – 7.30 p.m
{1 platoon from Nos 1. 2. 3. 4 Coy (O.C. Capt
{Bn. Hd. Qrs.   FREEMAN) – 7.35 p.m

5. R. Company 7th Batt. R. will arrive at Canadian Trench MG at 6.30 p.m. and will be distributed for instruction in the 4.

6. One days rations to be carried on the man

7. Officers kits and mens blankets to be ready for collection 2.30 p.m.

8. Receipts to pink for all Trench stores and copies of receipts sent to B. Hd Qrs for noon 12 th
Copy view of receipt to be noted [illegible] as o the [illegible].

9. The Bn will occupy Trenches as in attached schedule

10. Dressing Station R PEV NE Fm. N 34 b 0.
Batt. [illegible]
Batt. Hd Qrs TEA Fm.   N 34 a 4.5

Issued at 1 p.m.
Copy No 1   No 1 Co   [signature] Capt.
  -    2   2   Adjt. & OC
  -    3   3   Cheshire Rgt.
  -    4   4
  -    5   M.G.
  -    6   2 Lt. Jones
  7 Sgt Williams
  -    8   Lt. 7 Lancashire R.
  -    9   Lt. Suffolk R.
  -   10   Medical Officer
  -   11   Lt. [illegible]

Schedule of Trenches
No 1 Group.

No 1. Coy (less 1 platoon) + 1 platoon of Leicester R.
to relieve A Coy 1 Suffolk Reg.

    E 2   70 men + 1 M.G.   F. T.
    E 3   40 "   S. T.
    E 6   70 "   S. T.

    Total Garrison 180

No 2 Group.

No 3 Coy (less 1 platoon) + 1 platoon Leicester R.
to relieve C. Coy 1 Suffolk R.

    E 1   80 men   F. T.
    E 4   50 "   S. T.
    S P 7 25 men + 1 M.G. S. P.

    Total Garrison 155.

No 3 Group.

No 4 Coy (less 1 platoon) + 1 platoon Leicester R.
to relieve B. Coy 1 Suffolk R.

    No 15   150 men and 2 M.G.   F. T.
    15 S (Dugout) 40 men   S. T.

    Total Garrison 190.

No 4 Group.

No 2 Coy (less 1 platoon) + 1 Platoon Leicester R.
to relieve D Coy 1 Suffolk R.

    14 a   40 men   F. T.
    14 b. 70 "   S. T.
    14 S   40 "   S. T.

    Garrison 150

No 5 Group.
O. C. Capt. FREEMAN
1 platoon from Nos 1, 2, 3, 4 Coys to be in reserve at NIEUPORT DUGOUTS.

Regt'l Operation Order No 11
of 13-8-15

I. Reliefs will take place tonight as on attached schedule. O.C. 1 Coy 7 Leices'ters will come under orders of O.C. Cheshire Regt.

II. M.G. Detachments 7 Leicester Regt. will be attached to M.G. Detachment Cheshire Regt.

III. The following guides will be supplied at Bn. Hd. Qrs. at 4 P.M.
  1 Guide from Z.1. Z.2. Z.3. Z.6.
  1 Guide from M.G. Det. for each trench in which there are M.Gs.

4. Platoons of Nos. 2. 3. 4 Coys. at Newport dug-outs moving to trenches will be at Hd. Qrs. at 4.15 P.M. Nos. 2 & 4 will draw rations for themselves & Coys. when proceed to trenches.
O.C. No. 3 will make his own arrangements for drawing rations by sending party to Bn. Hd. Qrs. after 4.15 P.M.

5. No. 1 Coy. will obtain receipts for all stores handed over and send copies to Hd. Qrs. by 12 Noon tomorrow.

6. Reliefs to be reported by wire as soon as completed.

(Signed) A. R. Hill Capt
Adjutant Cheshire Regt

No. 1 copy to 1 Coy
 " 2   "   " 2
 " 3   "   " 3
 " 4   "   " 4
 " 5   "   7 Leicesters
 " 6   "   M.G.O.
 " 7   "   Adjutant
 " 8   "   Record

	FROM	TO	RELIEFING	AFTER RELIEF BY
(a) 1 Coy 7 Leicesters (b) No 2 Platoon	No. 1 Coy	LOCRE E 3	E2 E3 E6 E 4 Additional Garrison for O.C. No 3	No 1 Coy Cheshire	7 Leicesters
(c) No 3 Platoon	No 1 Coy	E 6	is Additional Garrison for O.C. No. 4		7 Leicesters
(d) No 1 Platoon	No 1 Coy	E 2	NEWPORT Dugouts		7 Leicesters
(e) No. 4 Platoon (f) No. 5 Platoon (g) No. 10 Platoon	No 1 Coy No 2 " No 3 "	Stand fast NEWPORT NEWPORT	at Newport in S E1	Platoon 7 Leicesters Platoon 7 Leicesters	
(h) Platoons 7 Leicesters with 1.2.3.4 Coys.		Trenches	Bn. H. Qrs.		A Cheshire Regt on arrival of additional Garrisons.

Copy No 8

2nd Cheshire Regiment   Copy No
Operation Order No 13. 18th August 1915.

1. The Battalion will be relieved by 1st Suffolk Regt tonight commencing on the left.

2. Bn. M.G. Detachments including Bomb Detachments in E2 will be relieved by M.G Detachments 1st Suffolk Regt before 8 pm.

3. O.C. Coys will send one guide per trench to Bn Hd Qtrs by 7 pm on 18th August.
   Guides for M.G will be detailed from Reserve teams at Bn Hd Qtrs.

4. One officer per Coy 1st Suffolk Regt will proceed in advance to trenches to take over stores etc. Copies of receipts for stores handed over to be sent to Orderly Room by 12 noon tomorrow – Attention is directed to G.R.O 899 copy attached. All grenades in future must be shewn under new nomenclature.

5. Coy's on relief will march independently to BADAJOS HUTS LOCRE reporting at Bn Hd Qtrs TEA FARM en route.

Copy No 1 to No 1
  -   2 - No 2
  -   3 - No 3
  -   4 - No 4
  -   5 - M.G.O
  -   6 - 2nd Mr + I.O
  -   7 - 1st Suffolk Regt
  -   8 - Retained.

Issued. 12 noon

R Hill Capt. Adj
2 Bn Ches R.

Grenades – Nomenclature of (G.R.O. 899) The nomenclature of grenades will now be as follows:—

Previous Nomenclature.	New Nomenclature
Service Hand Grenade (R.L. percussion, brass with cane handle & detonator).	Grenade, Hand No 1
Jonite or Mexican Hand Grenade (Hale's percussion pattern, brass with cane handle and detonator).	Grenade, Hand, No 2
Hale's Rifle Grenade (J.A. pattern with detonator).	Grenade .303 in short rifle, No 3.
Mills Hand Grenade (Iron oval shaped with safety fuze and detonator).	Grenade, Hand, No 5.
R.L. Grenade 1 lb (R.L. light friction pattern, tin, with friction igniter, safety fuze and detonator).	Grenade, Hand, No 6.
R.L. Grenade 2 lbs (R.L. heavy pattern, tin, with friction igniter, safety fuze and detonator).	Grenade, Hand, No 7.
Double Cylinder Light pattern Grenade (with No 8 detonator and safety fuze).	Grenade, Hand, No 8.
Double Cylinder Heavy pattern Grenade (with No 8 detonator and safety fuze).	Grenade, Hand, No 9
Hairbrush or Box Pattern Grenade (iron and steel with wood handle, with igniter, safety fuze, percussion and No 8 detonator).	Grenade, Hand, No 12.

Record

2nd Bn. Cheshire Regiment

Operation Orders d/ 24.8.15
by Lt Col. T.H.F. Pearse C.M.G. Comdg 2/Cheshire Rgt

(1) Reliefs will take place tomorrow night as follows:-

No 1 Group

14 'A' 40 F.T.
14 'B' 70 S.T.
14 'C' 40 S.T.
Total Garrison 150.

No 2 Coy. (less 15 men) Captn. Morton.

No 2 Group

15.   150
15 'S' 40
Total Garrison 190.

No 4 Coy. plus 15 men of No 2 Coy. Captn. Lloyd.

No 3 Group

E1   50
E3   40
E4   50
S.P 7 25
Total Garrison 165

No 1 Coy. Captn. Ogden.

Battalion Reserve.
No 3 Coy. Captn. Maxwell
in Nieuport Dug outs.

Machine Guns

2 Guns in 15
1 Gun in 'E' 2
1 Gun in S.P.7

2. Battalion Head Quarters will be at Tea Farm - Dressing Station at Dressing Farm

3. Machine Gun Detachment will parade at 4·0 pm (carrying their own rations) with Machine Gun limbers and will proceed via Dranoutre to day path to Tea Farm - N of Bus Farm - and relieve the Machine Guns of the Suffolk Regt.
Relief to be completed before 8·0 pm.

4. Company Commanders will proceed to the trenches to arrive at 6·0 pm and take over stores etc.
Company Sergt. Majors will accompany them.

(5) Battalion will march in the following order -
    No 1 No 4 No 2 No 3.
to march by Companies independently at 5 minutes interval.

    Head of Battn. will pass Battn. Head Quarters at 6.45 p.m.

Route. Dranoutre - Cross Roads N. of Bus Farm (halting places) to be reached by 8.15 p.m.

(6) One days rations to be carried on the man.

(7) Officer's Kits and mens blankets to be ready for collection at 2.30 p.m.

(8) Receipts to be given for all stores and copies of receipts sent to Battn. Hd Qrs. by 12 noon 26th. inst.
Completion of relief to be reported by wire as soon as completed.

                  A. R. Freeman Captain
                A/Adjutant of Cheshire Rgt.

The Officer Comdg,
  1st Bn Suffolk Regt.

Reference reliefs 25/26.

1. Machine Gun Detachment arrives 5-0 p.m. at path SOUTH of BUS FARM leading to 'T' FARM and proceeds to relieve Machine Gun Detachment of Suffolks.

2. Officers Comdg Companies will arrive in the trenches at 6-0 p.m. to take over from those of the Suffolk Regt.

3. Battn will arrive with transport at Cross Roads N of BUS FARM at 8-15 p.m.

4. Companies will proceed independently to relieve the trenches — as before — including E 3.

    No Guides will be required.

        Sgd T. H. Finch Pearse,
                                  Lieut Col
24th 8. 15.
        Comdg, 2/ Cheshire Regt,

2nd Cheshire Regiment　　　　Copy No

Operation Order No 14　　29th August 15.

<u>1</u>　The Battalion will be relieved by 1st Suffolk Regt tonight commencing on the left.

<u>2</u>　Bn M.G. Detachments including M.G. Detachment in E2 will be relieved by M.G. Detachment 1st Suffolk Regt before 8 p.m.

<u>3</u>　O.C. Coys will send one guide per trench to Bn Hd Qrs by 7 p.m on 29th August.
　　Guides for M.G. will be detailed from Reserve teams at Bn Hd Qrs

<u>4</u>　One officer per Coy 1st Suffolk Regt will proceed in advance to trenches to take over stores etc. Copies of receipts for stores handed over to be sent to Orderly Room by 12 noon tomorrow.

<u>5</u>　Coys on relief will march independently to BADAJOS HUTS LOCRE reporting at Bn Hd Qtrs Tea Farm en route.

　　　　　　　(Sgd) N.R. Truman Capt
　　　　　　　　　2/ Cheshire Regt.

Sheet II

"D" Coy & 1 platoon "A" Coy.
    15   150 Rifles
    15.S.   40 "
     Total 190 "

"C" Coy   14 a   40 rifles
     14 b   70 "
     14 S   40 "
     Total 150 "

The above numbers do not include:-
Bombers, Signallers or Stretcher Bearers.
2 platoons "A" Coy & details.
Battn: Reserve Nieuport dug-outs.

5. One guide per company. From 2nd Cheshire Regt will meet the Battn. at T. Farm. at 7-30 pm.

7. The usual relief reports will be rendered.

8. The Battn will march at 6.15 pm.
Starting Point:-
   South end of "D" Coy Huts on Main Road.
Order of March:-
  "B" Coy & 1 platoon "A" Coy.
  "D" " & 1 "   "A" "
  "C"
  2 platoons "A" Company & Details.
     (Sd) J. A. White Lt Col.
     Comdg' Suffolk Regt

<u>Secret</u>
Operation Order W20 by:-
Lieut Col: H A White DSO
Commanding Suffolk Regiment
29-8-1915.

1. The Battalion will relieve the 2-nd Cheshire Regt in the trenches tonight.
2. The Machine gun detachment will relieve the Machine guns of 2-nd Cheshire Regt including the detachment in E 2. This afternoon. Relief to be completed by 8 pm and all relieved garrisons to be clear of the Communication Trenches by that hour.
3. One officer per Company and Company Sergt Majors will proceed to the trenches this afternoon to arrive there before 6. pm to take over trenches. Receipts will be given and received for all Trench Stores taken over. These receipts will be handed to the adjutant by 11 am tomorrow morning
4. Companies will be distributed in the Trenches as under:-

"B" Company ∇ 1 platoon "A" Coy
E 1   80 rifles
E 4   50 "
E 3   40 "
S P Y 1 Off 25 "
Total <u>195</u>

2 Ches O.O. No 14   Copy No

Ref. Map 28.   31. 8. 15

1. Bn will move to KEMMEL SHELTERS
   to-day.

2. Order of march. 1. 2. 3. 4   HQ & M.G. Det.
   Starting point.   Orderly Room.
   Route   via de BRULOOZE
   CABt (M 24 a 9.4)
   Companies will march at 15 min
   interval
   No 1 Coy will pass starting point at 3.30 p.m.

3. Blankets will be taken.
   Carts for loading will be at BADAJOZ
   HUTS 2.30 p.m.
   Transport will follow HQ & M.G. Det
   at 15 min interval.

4. Coy Commanders will report at O.R.
   that their lines are clean on parting

5. Reg. Q.M. Sergt. will arrange to take over shelter
   stores at KEMMEL SHELTERS
   this morng.
   Copy No 1. Circulated to   R Hunter.
              O.C. Coys M.S.   Adjt 2 Ches R
              Qr.M.
        2 Retained.
        Issued 10.45 AM.

84th Bde.
28th Div.

2nd CHESHIRES

SEPTEMBER

1915

On His Majesty's Service.

Army Form C. 2118.

WAR DIARY
or
INTELLIGENCE SUMMARY.
(Erase heading not required.)

Instructions regarding War Diaries and Intelligence Summaries are contained in F. S. Regs., Part II, and the Staff Manual respectively. Title pages will be prepared in manuscript.

Hour, Date, Place.	Summary of Events and Information.	Remarks and references to Appendices.
9. A.M. 1 September. KEMMEL SHELTERS	No 1 Coy formed Brigade fatigues of 50 men.	P.H
7 A.M - 12.30 P.M 2 Sept.	Paraded under Coy Commanders for drill, musketry and physical training	P.H
4. P.M. " "	Men put into dug-outs for ½ hour as Germans dropped a few shells over KEMMEL HILL	P.H
7 P.M " "	Bn left to take over trenches from 1st SUFFOLK Regt.	Bde. O.O. 50
10.50 P.M. " "	Relief completed - Heavy rain.	Regt. O.O. 15
TRENCHES near LINDENHOEK 3 Sept.		
12 noon	Casualties previous 24 hours nil. S.A.A. expended 1016 rounds. Raining hard. Lieut WATSON proceeded on leave.	P.H
9 A.M. 4 Sept.	2 Lieut ADSHEAD left to join Brigade trench mortar Germans shelled S.P. 7.	
10 A.M " "	Lieut Col PEARSE from act. Bol. Jer. assumed command of Bn.	
11 A.M. " "	P.H	
12 noon " "	Lieut McGREGOR + 16 O.R. to 2 Coy left to form Brigade Drainage section	
1.30 P.M. " "	O.C. in E 1 reports Germans heard working above our own. Brigade trench Officer sent for - no results. Casualties Nil.	P.H

WAR DIARY
or
INTELLIGENCE SUMMARY.
(Erase heading not required.)

Army Form C. 2118.

Instructions regarding War Diaries and Intelligence Summaries are contained in F. S. Regs., Part II, and the Staff Manual respectively. Title pages will be prepared in manuscript.

Hour, Date, Place.	Summary of Events and Information.	Remarks and references to Appendices.
TRENCHES NEAR LINDENHOEK 6 Sept		
11.30 p.m. 6 Sept	We exploded mine near D4. Germans opened rapid fire which was returned. Our casualts accounted in E1 trench.	R
4 p.m. " "	O.C. No 1 reported that L/C Capper and Pte McBride from sap in rear of E1 shot two German Officers who were exposing themselves 50 yds off. They had unbraided collars and peaked caps with red tops. Casualties nil.	R.H.
" "		R.H.
10 am 7 Sept	No 2 Coy heavy shelled about 180 shells twice fired. No casualties	
5 p.m " "	Lt Col PEARSE took over temporary command of the Brigade. Major RODDY command of the Bⁿ.	R.H
Night 8·9	Battⁿ relieved J 1ˢᵗ Suffolk Rgt - on relief Bⁿ proceeded to KEMMEL SHELTERS	
2 p.m 9 Sept LOCRE	Bⁿ. marched to BADAJOS HUTS LOCRE	
8 p.m	Parade for men from J Div⁹ concert party	R.H

Army Form C. 2118.

WAR DIARY
or
INTELLIGENCE SUMMARY.
(Erase heading not required.)

Instructions regarding War Diaries and Intelligence Summaries are contained in F. S. Regs., Part II, and the Staff Manual respectively. Title pages will be prepared in manuscript.

Hour, Date, Place.	Summary of Events and Information.	Remarks and references to Appendices.
LOIRE		
7-12 noon 10¹ Sept.	Ranges allotted to Bn for training of young men drafted shot	PM
7.20 P.M. 11¹ Sept.	Test alarm. Bn turned out in 40 min. 1ˢᵗ Line transport ready to move in 55 min.	PM
10 A.M. 12 Sept.	Church of England Service for troops in LOIRE	PM
2.30 P.M. " "	Bn marched to KEMMEL SHELTERS	
	2 Lieut RIMINGTON returned from Bombay class.	
Night 13-14 Sept.	Battⁿ relieved 1ˢᵗ Suffolk Regt in trenches Relief commenced 7 p.m ended 10.55 p.m.	PM
TRENCHES near LINDENHOEK		
11.30 A.M. 15 Sept.	5 casualties in No 3 Coy owing to one of our H.E. Shells falling short	
9. P.M. " "	Draft of 107 men arrived from ENGLAND Capt PHILLIPS & Lt BIRKET hitherto Army reports for 24 hrs instruction	B.TO.P 53} R. O. O. 76.}
10 A.M. 16 "	Lieut JONES proceeded on leave.	PM
3 P.M. 16 "	Officers Mess Instruction Class out of trenches	
4 P.M. 16 "	Lt COLE left for 1 days M. G. course at WISQUES	PM

Army Form C. 2118.

WAR DIARY
or
INTELLIGENCE SUMMARY.
(Erase heading not required.)

Instructions regarding War Diaries and Intelligence Summaries are contained in F. S. Regs., Part II, and the Staff Manual respectively. Title pages will be prepared in manuscript.

Hour, Date, Place.	Summary of Events and Information.	Remarks and references to Appendices.
Trenches near LINDENHOEK		
4 p.m. 17th Sept	Our 9.2, 4.5 + field guns bombarded BLACK REDOUBT - SPANBROEK MOLEN 4 hours in front of our left trenches. Germans quickly retaliated and garrison of supporting point were obliged to go into shell trenches. One slight casualty as result of retaliation.	P.H.
10.30 A.M 18th Sept.	Information received that 28th Divn would withdraw & be replaced by a Canadian Divn.	
7.30 p.m - 9.30 pm 20 Sept	Bnys fr of Canadian Bn with trenches. Lieut COLE returned from M.G. course.	P.H.
L'OTRE		
8.30 A.M 21 Sept.	Relief of Bn by Canadians. Bn on relief proceed to L'OTRE.	P.H.
BORRE	Battn marched at 8.30am & billeted at BORRE distance about 10 miles - 16 men fell out. Bn had first casualties in the Brigade.	P.H.
23 Sept.	Battn rent marched by companies - exercises of tuis spoer in their district physical training.	P.H.
2 p.m. 24 Sept	Battn route march.	P.H.
25 Sept	Battn on duty	
9.30 AM 25 Sept.	Battn route march.	P.H.

Army Form C. 2118.

WAR DIARY
or
INTELLIGENCE SUMMARY.
(Erase heading not required.)

Instructions regarding War Diaries and Intelligence Summaries are contained in F. S. Regs., Part II, and the Staff Manual respectively. Title pages will be prepared in manuscript.

Hour, Date, Place.	Summary of Events and Information.	Remarks and references to Appendices.
BORRE		
7 p.m. 25 Sept	Bn warned to hold itself in readiness to arm by train from HAARZEBROOK at 2 hours notice	RA
5 A.M. 26 Sept	Orders received to march with other troops in the Brigade area at 9 A.M. from Brigade starting point	
8.15 AM 26 Sept	Batt. left billets & joined column marching as rear Bn of the Brigade.	
1 P.M. " "	Batt. arrived at PARADISE about 2 miles S. of MERVILLE and halted for dinner.	
2 P.M.	Orders received to arm to HINGES at 3 p.m.	
3 P.M.	Orders to arm on HINGES cancelled. Bn went into billets near PARADISE.	RA
9 A.M. 27 Sept	Entrained in 37 lorries for BETHUNE	
SAILLY-LA-BOURSE		
1.30 P.M. " "	Detrained at BETHUNE and marched in Brigade to SAILLY-LA-BOURSE which was reached at 1.30 p.m. Batt. bivouacked in field.	
6. P.M. " "	Bn. went into billets at SAILLY-LA-BOURSE. Raining hard.	RA
28 Sept	Remained in same billets.	RA
11 A.M. 29 Sept	Bn remains in billets - Brigade detailed as reserve to 1 Corps	RA 8. OO 62.

Army Form C. 2118.

WAR DIARY
or
INTELLIGENCE SUMMARY.
(Erase heading not required.)

Instructions regarding War Diaries and Intelligence Summaries are contained in F. S. Regs., Part II, and the Staff Manual respectively. Title pages will be prepared in manuscript.

Hour, Date, Place.	Summary of Events and Information.	Remarks and references to Appendices.
SAILLY-LA-BOURSE 3.30 p.m. 29th Septr.	Battalion marched to ANNEQUIN and billeted. Heavy rain	
ANNEQUIN 9 a.m. 30th Septr.	Battalion practised in throwing bombs & grenades	
5.30 p.m. " "	Bn proceeded to trenches via VERMELLES and took over from Royal Fusiliers, No 1 and No 2 Companies in the WEST FACE of the HOHENZOLLERN REDOUBT, No 3 and 4 Companies in Support.	

11/10/15

[signature] Major
Comndg 2nd Bn. The Cheshire Regt

2 Ches R. O.O. No 15 Copy No
1. 9. 15.

1. On night 2/3 Sept. Bn will relieve 1st
Suffolk Reg. in the trenches, and their
machine guns. Distribution attached.

2. Coy Commanders + S. Majors will proceed
in advance reach T FARM by 5 p.m
to take over trenches

3. Signallers will be relieved by 4 p.m.
Guards will be relieved by 4 P.M.
Machine guns will relieve Machine guns
of SUFFOLK R before 8 p.m.

4. Companies will pass the O.R as under
No 1 Coy + 1 platoon no 4   7. 0 P.M.
No 3 Coy + 1 platoon No 4 Coy 7. 5 p.m.
No 2 Coy   7. 10 p.m.
No 4 Coy less 1 platoon   7. 15 p.m.
One guide per Trench from 1st Suffolk
R will meet Coys at T. FARM.

5. Officers Kits and mens Blankets to be
ready for collection 3 p.m.

6. Copies of receipts for french stores to be at Bn HQ pro 12 noon 3 Sep.

7. Usual ~~receipts~~ reports to be present.

R Hunter Adj.
2 Ches R.

No 1 to No 1 Coy.
- 2 - - 2 -
- 3 - - 3 -
- 4 - - 4 -
- 5 - M.O. T.O. Qr mr
- 6 - 1 Suffolk R.
- 7 } Retained
- 8

Trench Strengths.
Minimum Garrisons

No 1 group - No 1 Coy + 1 platoon No 4

E 1   ~~350~~ 90
E 3   40
E 4   50
S.P. 7   25
         ~~115~~ 205

No 2 group No ~~2~~ 3 Coy + 1 platoon No 4 Coy

14a 15   150
     15 S   40
                190

No 3 group. No 2 Coy 1
14 a   40
14 b   70
14 S   40
             150

NEWPORT DUG-OUTS

No 4 Coy less 2 Platoon.

R Hill Lor Adj 2 Cheo R.

Amended Schedule

No 1 group No 1 Coy.

E 1	80 men	} No 4 Coy + 16 men from No 2
E 3	40 "	
E 4	50 "	
	170	

No 2 group No 3 Coy.

15	100	} No 7 Coy + 15 men from No 2 2 M.G.
15 S	60	
	160	

No 3 group

14 a	50	70	} No 3 Coy
14 b.	50	40	148
14 S	40	30	
	140		

S.P. 7.   25 men 1 officer No 4 Coy.   1 MG.
½ E 6.   35 men 1 officer No 4 Coy.
~~Regnt~~ Newport Dusonés Renaudi No 4

S P 8.   1 M G.

No 1 Coy
35 men No 4 Coy for garrison ½ E 6 } 7 p.m.

No 3 Coy
25 men No 4 Coy for garrison S.P 7 } 7.5 p.m.

No 2 Coy.   7.10 p.m.

No 4 Coy less 60 men   7.15 p.m.

Guide for 15 & 15 S will be at T FARM
7.30 p.m.

35 men NO 4 Coy for E 6 will
come under Command of O. NO 1 Coy

2 Ches R. O.O. no 16.   Copy No

9. 9. 15

1. The Bn. & M.G. Sectⁿ on relief to-night by 1ˢᵗ Suffolk Reg. will march direct under Coy & M.G. Commanders to KEMMEL SHELTERS reporting at Bn H.Q. en route.

2. 1 Guide per trench Coy will be at Bⁿ HD Qrs 7 . p. m.

3. All water cans + dixies will be at advanced ration dump of 4 p.m & will be carried down by a fatigue party from No 4 Coy.

4. Machine guns will be relieved before 8 p.m.

5. Copies of handing over receipts to be sent to Adjⁿ before 12 noon on 9ᵗʰ.

R Stin Capt & Major
Adj

2 Ches R. O.O. No 17 Cops 8
12. 9. 15.

1. The Batt" will move to KEMMEL SHELTERS to-day marching via de BRULOOZE Cab'

2. Companies will march at 15 min interval - No 1 Coy at 2.30 p.m and remainder in succession. O.C Coys will report at O. Room before leaving. M G Det will follow B" "A"

3. Blankets etc will be ready for collection by 1 p.m.

4. Coy Q. M. Sgt will proceed in advance to take over shelters & huts.
Coy No 1 to No 1.
 - 2 - No 2
 - 3 - No 3
 - 4 - No 4
 - 5 - M G O
 - 6 - T. or Q. M.
7 + 8. Retained.

R/Hu hay + Adj'
2 Bn Cheshire R

2nd Battalion Cheshire Regt.
Operation Order No 18
dated 13th. 9. 15.

__1__ On night 14/15 September Battalion will relieve 1st Suffolk Regt in the trenches and their machine guns Distribution attached.

__2__ Coy Commanders + Sergt Majors will proceed in advance, to reach 'T' Farm by 5 p.m to take over trenches.

__3__ Signallers will be relieved by 4 p.m Guards will be relieved by 2.50 p.m. Machine Guns will relieve Machine Guns of Suffolk Regt before 8 p.m.

__4__ Companies will pass the O. Room as under.
    No 4 Coy + 7 men No 1 Coy   7 p.m
    No 3 Coy   7.5 p.m.
    No 1 Coy less 7 men   7.10 p.m
    No 2 Coy less 2 officers + 60 men 7.15 p.m
One guide per trench from 1st Suffolk Regt will meet Coys at T Farm

5. Officers Kits + mens blankets to be ready for collection at 3 p.m.

6. Copies of receipts for trench Stores to be at Battn Hd Qtrs 12 noon 15th September.

7. Usual reports to be sent.

8. No 2 Coy will detail 20 men to assist Machine Gunners in taking ammunition to trenches. Time of parade to be arranged with Machine Gun Officer.

        Sgd R. R. Freeman, Capt
        A/ Adjt, 2/ Cheshire Regt.

No 1 to No 1 Coy
= 2   = 2 =
= 3   = 3 =
= 4   = 4 =
= 5   M.G.O. T.O. 2r Mr
= 6   1st Suffolk Regt
= 7 } Retained
= 8 }

Trench Strength
Minimum Garrisons

No 1 Group No 4 Coy plus 7 men No 1 Coy

  E 1 80
  E 3 40
  E 4 <u>50</u>
     170

No 2 Group No 3 Coy

 15 F.T 100 2 M.G.
 15 S   <u>60</u>
     160

No 3 Group No 1 Coy less 7 men

 14 A 70
 14 B 40
 14 S <u>30</u>
    140

S.P. 7 :- 1 Officer & 25 men No 2 Coy   } 1 M.G.
   Parade with & under command No 3 Coy }

½ E 6 - 1 Officer & 35 men No 2 Coy
   Parade with & under command No 4 Coy }

Nieuport Dugout 77 men No 2 Coy

S.P. 8 1 M.G

      Sgd R. R. Freeman Capt
      A/ Adjt, 2/ Cheshire Regt.

2nd Cheshire Regt. Operation Orders
by Major E L. Roddy. 19/9/15

No 20

1. On the night of the 20th/21st Sept 1915 the Battn will be relieved by the 13th Canadian Battn (Royal Highlanders)

2. Guides will be provided by Companies and Machine Guns as follows —

No 1 Company.	14 A	2
	14 B	2 2/Lt K. Smith
	14 S	2
No 3 Company.	15	2
	15 S	2
	SP 7	2
No 4 Company	E 1	2
	E 3	2
	E 4	2
	E 6	2
No 2 Company	Hunfort A.O.	2
Machine Guns :—	SP 8	1
	15	2
	SP 7	1

Company Guides will report to the Adjutant T Farm at 6 pm and those of the machine Guns at 4 pm

3. Guides will be in possession of a piece of paper showing what trench they are guides for.

4. Receipts will be obtained for all Trench Stores handed over. These receipts to be handed into the Orderly Room by 9 am 21st inst.

5. Camp Kettles – Regimental Property – will be sent to T Farm not later than 7.30 pm

6. On relief Companies will proceed to Locrehoff Farm via Dranoutre, Company Commanders reporting at T Farm, en route.

N.R. Freeman Captⁿ
a/Adjt Welsh R.

Comdg. Offr. Cheshire Regt 26·9·14:—

1. 15 Brigade will march to Merville morning 26th September 1914.

2. Route Petit Sec Bois – LA RUE DU BOIS – Vieux Bergain, – Nieu Bergain to Merville.

3. Starting Point of Brigade. Road junction just West of P in Petit Sec Bois.
   2d Cheshire Regt 8·45 a.m.

4. Battalion will march in following order
   Signallers, Grenadiers,
   No 4 Company
   " 1
   " 2
   " 3

   Starting Point Mairie W of No 3 Co's billets
   Time 8 am

5. No 3 Company will furnish a party of 20 NCOs and Men with fixed bayonets who will march in rear of the Brigade and collect all stragglers.
   This party will be in charge of Major

6. Billeting Party under 2/Lt M: Bergne will meet Staff Captain at Road Junction due W of Bn LA Brienne (3 mile NE of Merville) at 7·15 am.

7. Remainder of 1st line Transport will form up in order of march in units head rear of X Roads just South of M in

Bod dulles by 5.27 am Thence to
starting Point

A R Newman Captain
a/Adjt 1/Cheshire Regt

OPERATION ORDER No.59   Copy No.4
by
Brigadier-General T.H.Finch-Pearse, C.M.G.,   Secret
Commanding 84th Infantry Brigade.

20th September 1915.

Reference Map Hazebrouck 5a
1/100,000 Belgium & France
Sheet 2a 1/40,000.

1. On the 21st September the Brigade leaves its present area for the neighbourhood of PRADELLES.

Route LOCRE - BAILLEUL thence along road turning to the South just West of BAILLEUL near bridge over BECQUE DE LA FLANCHE - MOOLENACKER.

2. Starting point - Cross-roads square M 2a c 9.0.

Order of March:-

Band	...	9 a.m.
Signalling Section.	...	9 a.m.
2nd Cheshire Regiment.	...	9.2 a.m.
Brigade H.Q.Transport.	...	9.10 a.m.
2nd Northd:Fusiliers.	...	9.12 a.m.
1st Welch Regiment.	...	9.20 a.m.
6th Welch Regiment.	...	9.28 a.m.
1st Suffolk Regiment.	...	9.35 a.m.

Baggage & Supply wagons march at 1 p.m. under orders of O.C., No. 3 Company, A.S.C.

3. All 1st Line & Train transport (except such 1st Line Transport not required by 1st Suffolk Regt at their billets, which will remain in its transport lines & join the Regiment as it passes) will join its unit and be clear of the main roads by 9.30 a.m.

4. 25th Field Ambulance will detail 1 M.O. and 2 Field Ambulances to follow in rear of Brigade.

S C Gepp
Major,
Brigade Major,
84th Infantry Brigade.

Issued at 1 p.m.

No.1 Retained.
No.2 2nd Northd:Fusiliers.
No.3 1st Suffolk Regt.
No.4 2nd Cheshire Regt.
No.5 1st Welch Regt.
No.6 6th Welch Regt.
No.7 28th Division.
No.8 No.3 Coy, A.S.C.
No.9 25th Field Ambulance.

Operation order No. 50   Copy No. 4

by

Lieutenant-Colonel T.H.Finch-Pearse, C.M.G.,

Commanding 84th Infantry Brigade.

1st September 1915.

Secret – not to be taken to trenches

1. On the night of 1st/2nd September 1st Monmouth Regiment will relieve their garrisons and machine guns in S.P.s 8 and 9.

2. On the night of 2nd/3rd September 2nd Cheshire Regiment will relieve 1st Suffolk Regiment and their machine guns.

3. On the night of 3rd/4th September 6th Welch Regiment will relieve the two companies in the trenches and the machine guns in F.2 and F.4.

E.C. Gepp.

Major,
Brigade Major,
84th Infantry Brigade.

Issued at 4-45 p.m.

No.1 Retained.
No.2 2nd Northd-Fusiliers.
No.3 1st Suffolk Regt.
No.4 2nd Cheshire Regt.
No.5 1st Welch Regt.
No.6 1st Monmouth Regt.
No.7 6th Welch Regt.
No.8 31st Brigade, R.F.A.
No.9 Supply Officer, 84th Inf.Bde.

OPERATION ORDER No.51   Copy No. 4

by

Lieutenant-Colonel T.H.Finch-Pearse, C.M.G.,

Commanding 94th Infantry Brigade.

Secret

2nd September 1915.

1. The garrisons of S.Ps 8 and 9 found by 1st Monmouth Regt will be withdrawn today.

2. The distribution and garrisons of the trenches held by Brigade will be in accordance with the attached Schedule..

3. The machine guns and teams in G.3, G.1, F.5, F.4 will be found by the left Battalion. Those in F.2, E.2, S.P. 9 and S.P.10 by the Centre Battalion. Those in S.P.8, 15 (2 machine guns and teams) and S.P.7 by the Right Battalion.

4. The necessary adjustment will be completed by 7 p.m. tonight and a report made to this office by all units concerned.

Issued at .... 11 a.m.

E. Gepp.
Major,
Brigade Major,
94th Infantry Brigade.

No.1 Retained.
No.2 2nd Northd:Fusiliers.
No.3 1st Suffolk Regt.
No.4 2nd Cheshire Regt.
No.5 1st Welch Regt.
No.6 1st Monmouth Regt.
No.7 6th Welch Regt.
No.8 31st Brigade, R.F.A.

Trench.	Garrison	Remarks.	Held by.
G.3	70 & 1 M.G.		
G.3 Suppt.	40		
G.2	65		
G.2 Suppts	30		LEFT.
G.1	50 & 1 M.G.		RIGHT
G.1 Suppts	30		
F.5	70 & 1 M.G.		BATTALIONS
F.5 Suppts.	40	To be known as F.7.	
F.4	70 & 1 M.G.		
F.4 Suppts	40	To be known as F.6 right.	
S.P.10	25 & 1 M.G.		
S.P. 9	30 & 1 M.G.		
		Remainder in Kemmel Schools.	
F.2	75 & 1 M.G.		
F.2 Suppts	40	To be known as F.6 left.	
E.2	40 & 1 M.G.		
E.2 Suppts	20	To be known as E.7	CENTRE
½ E.6	35		BATTALION.
S.P.8	25 & 1 M.G.		
		Remainder in Regent St. Dugouts.	
½ E.6	35 ✗		
E.3	40 ✓		
E.1	80 ✗		
E.4	50 ✓		
15	100 & 2 M.Gs ✓		RIGHT
15 S	60 ✗	Trench to be fit for occupation by 6th inst.	BATTALION.
14a	50 ✓		
14b	50 ✗		
14s	40 ✓		
S.P.7	25 & 1 M.G.		

Remainder in NEWPORT DUGOUTS.

OPERATION ORDER No.52   Copy No.4

by

Brigadier-General L.J.Bols, C.B., D.S.O.,

Commanding 84th Infantry Brigade.

Secret
Not to be taken
into the trenches

4th September 1915.

On the night of 5th/6th instant the 2nd Battalion Northumberland Fusiliers will relieve the 1st Battalion Welch Regiment and their Machine-Guns.

Issued at 11.17 a.m.

E C Gepp
Major,
Brigade Major,
84th Infantry Brigade.

No.1 Retained.
No.2 2nd Northd:Fusiliers.
No.3 1st Suffolk Regt.
No.4 2nd Cheshire Regt.
No.5 1st Welch Regt.
No.6 6th Welch Regt.
No.7 83rd Infty:Bde.
No.8 31st Brigade, R.F.A.
No.9 Supply Officer, 84th Bde.

Copy No. 4

OPERATION ORDER No. 83
by
Brigadier-General L.J.Bols, C.B., D.S.O.,
Commanding 84th Infantry Brigade.

Secret

Not to be taken into the trenches

7th September 1915.

1. On the night of 8th/9th instant 1st Suffolk Regiment will relieve 2nd Cheshire Regiment and their machine guns.

2. On the night of 9th/10th instant 6th Welch Regiment will relieve the two companies in the trenches.

Issued at _____

E c Gepp.
Major,
Brigade Major,
84th Infantry Brigade.

No. 1 Retained.
No. 2 2nd Northd: Fusiliers.
No. 3 1st Suffolk Regt.
No. 4 2nd Cheshire Regt. —
No. 5 1st Welch Regt.
No. 6 6th Welch Regt.
No. 7 31st Brigade, R.F.A.
No. 8 Supply Officer, 84th Bde.

OPERATION ORDER No.54
by
Lieut:Colonel T.H.Finch-Pearse, C.M.G.,
Commanding 84th Infantry Brigade.

Copy No. 4

Secret

Not to be taken into the trenches

10th September 1915.

On the night of 11th/12th instant 1st Battalion Welch Regiment will relieve 2nd Battalion Northumberland Fusiliers and their machine guns.

Issued at 11.30 a.m.

E.C. Gepp
Major,
Brigade Major,
84th Infantry Brigade.

No.1 retained.
No.2 2nd Northd:Fusiliers.
No.3 1st Suffolk Regt.
No.4 2nd Cheshire Regt.
No.5 1st Welch Regt.
No.6 6th Welch Regt.
No.7 31st Brigade, R.F.A.
No.8 Supply Officer, 84th Bde.

OPERATION ORDER No.55
by
Lieutenant-Colonel T.H.Finch Pearse, C.M.G.,
Commanding 84th Infantry Brigade,
11th Sepetmber 1915.

Not to be taken into the trench

Secret

1. The following paragraph will be substituted for paragraph 5 of Operation Order No. 45.

Begins:-

    5. Battalions at rest will be prepared to move at 40 minutes notice at any time.

1st Line Transport will also be ready to move and will await orders in the transport lines.

                                                  E C Gepp Major,
                                                  Brigade Major,
                                           84th Infantry Brigade.

Issued at 12.30 p.m.

No.1 retained.
No.2 2nd N.Fuslrs.
No.3 1st Suffolk Regt.
No.4 2nd Cheshire Regt.
No.5 1st Welch Regt.
No.6 6th Welch Regt.
No.7 84th Bde. M.G.Officer.
No.8 84th Bde Signals.
No.9 31st Brigade, R.F.A.

OPERATION ORDER No.56
by
Lieutenant-Colonel T.H.Finch-Pearse, C.M.G.,
Commanding 84th Infantry Brigade.

Copy No. 4

Secret

13th September 1915.

1. On the night of 14th/15th inst: 2nd Cheshire Regiment will relieve 1st Suffolk Regiment, and their machine guns.

2. On the night of 15th/16th September 6th Welch Regiment will relieve their two companies in the trenches.

Not to be taken into the trenches

E.C. Gepp.
Major,
Brigade Major,
84th Infantry Brigade.

Issued at 1-15 p.m.

No.1 retained.
No.2 2nd Northd:Fuslrs.
No.3 1st Suffolk Regt.
No.4 2nd Cheshire Regt.
No.5 1st Welch Regt.
No.6 6th Welch Regt.
No.7 31st Brigade, R.F.A.
No.8 Supply Officer, 84th Bde.

OPERATION ORDER No. 57.   Copy No......

by

Lieut-Colonel Finch-Pearse, C.M.G.,   Secret

Commanding 84th Infantry Brigade.

16th September 1915.

Not to be taken into the trenches

1. On the night of the 17/18th instant the 2nd Northd: Fusiliers will relieve the 1st Welch Regiment and their Machine Guns.

2. On the same night the 2nd Cheshire Regiment will take over half E.6 from 6th Welch Regiment.

The garrison of E.6 will be reduced to 50.

Issued at ...6.20p.m...

E C Gepp
Major,
Brigade Major,
84th Infantry Brigade.

No.1. Retained.
No.2. 2nd Northd: Fusiliers.
No.3. 1st Suffolk Regiment.
No.4. 2nd Cheshire Regiment.
No.5. 1st Welch Regiment.
No.6. 6th Welch Regiment.
No.7. 31st Brigade R.F.A.
No.8. Supply Officer 84th Bde:

No. 268

Confidential

To:-
2nd Cheshire Regt.

On the morning of the 19th instant, Officers from the 3rd Canadian Brigade will go into the trenches held by this Brigade, for 24 hours.

The guides to meet the officers will be the same as those who will meet the Canadian Battalions on the night of the relief. The guides will be in possession of a piece of paper showing what trench they are guides for.

When guiding up the officers the route to be taken is as shown on attached table, which is also the route to be taken on the night of the reliefs.

E.C. Gepp
Major,
Brigade Major,
84th Infantry Brigade.

18th Sept:1915.

Guides.	Trench.	Guides for trench.	Guides for M.G.
Under the command of 1 officer 2nd N. Fus: Locre Barrier N 19 d 7.4 at 10 a.m. and thence by VIA GELLIA.	G.3	2	1
	G.3s	2	
	G.2	2	
	G.2s	2	
	G.1	2	1
	G.1s	2	
Under the command of 1 officer 2nd N. Fusiliers Locre Barrier N 19 d 7.4 at 10 a.m. and thence via REGENT ST.& PALL MALL.	F.5	2	1
	F.7	2	
	F.4	2	1
	F.6 left	2	
	S.P.10	2	1
	S.P.9	2	1
Under an officer 6th Welch Regt. Locre Barrier N 19 d 7.4 at 10 a.m. and thence via REGENT STREET & PALL MALL.	F.2	2	1
	F.6 right	2	
Under an officer of 6th Welch Regt. at road junction Square N 33 c 9.7 at 10 a.m. thence via REGENT ST. & PALL MALL.	E.2	2	1
	S.P.8	2	1
Under an officer 2nd Cheshire Regt. at Road Junction Square N 33 c 9.7. at 10a.m. thence via REGENT ST. VIGO ST.& PICADILLY.	E.6	2	
	E.1	2	
	E.3	2	
Under an officer 2nd Cheshire Regt. at Square N 33 d 9.7 at 10a.m. and thence via KINGSWAY.	E.4	2	2
	15	2	
	15s	2	
	14a	2	
	14b	2	
	14s	2	
	S.P.7	2	1

OPERATION ORDER No.58   Copy No. 4

by

Brigadier-General T.H.Finch-Pearse, C.M.G.,

Commanding 84th Infantry Brigade.

Secret

19th September 1915.

Reference Map Belgium &
France, Sheet 2a 1/40,000.

1. On the night 20th/21st Sept: the line now held by the Brigade will be handed over to the 3rd Canadian Infantry Brigade.

2. Trenches 14a to E.2 inclusive with their support trenches & S.P.7 & 8, will be relieved by the 13th Canadian Battalion (Royal Highlanders), and trenches F.2 to G.3 with their Support trenches and S.P.9 & 10 by the 16th Canadian Infantry Battalion.

3. Guides will be provided by Battalions in the trenches in accordance with instructions No.269 dated 18th inst. Guides for machine guns to be at the Locre Barrier square N 19 d 7.4 and road junction square N 33 c 9.7 at 4.30 p.m. and guides for the relieving Canadian Battalions at the Locre Barrier at 6.30 p.m. and at square N 33 c 9.7 at 7 p.m.

4. On relief, Brigade Headquarters to Locre. 2nd Northd:Fus: and 2 companies 6th Welch Regt via Locre Barrier to Locre, 2nd Cheshire Regt via Dranoutre to Locrehoff Farm.

5. 1st Suffolk Regt will vacate Kemmel Shelters by 5.30 p.m. 20th instant.

E C Gepp

Major,
Brigade Major,
84th Infantry Brigade.

Issued at 7.45 p.m.

No.1 Retained.
~~No.2 2nd Northd:Fusiliers.~~
~~No.3 2nd Cheshire Regt.~~
~~No.4 1st Welch Regt.~~
No.2 2nd N.Fusiliers.
No.3 1st Suffolk Regt.
No.4 2nd Cheshire Regt.
No.5 1st Welch Regt.
No.6 6th Welch Regt.
No.7 31st Brigade R.F.A.
No.8 38th Field Coy:R.E.
No.9 3rd Canadian Infty:Bde.
No.10 No.3 Coy:A.S.C.
No.11 28th Division.

1. Brigade Billeting area is as follows.

Northern Boundary from ROUGE CROIX (inclusive) to BORRE (inclusive) thence along HAZEBROUCK road to HAZEBROUCK-CAESTRE Railway.

Western boundary from last point to Railway junction with HAZEBROUCK-BAILLEUL Railway.

Southern boundary from last point going east along HAZEBROUCK - BAILLEUL Railway to point where road crosses railway just North of B in PLATE BECQUE.

Eastern boundary along last named road going North to the first E in PRADELLES thence East to ROUGE CROIX - STRAZEELE Road thence to ROUGE CROIX.

2. The following will be taken as Standing Orders for marches:-

(a) Battalions will on no account form up on main roads nor will their transport stand on main roads whilst getting ready to move off.

(b) The Officer Commanding the rear Battalion will detail 1 officer and 20 Other Ranks with fixed bayonets to march in rear of the Brigade and bring along all stragglers. A report will be rendered to Brigade H.Q. with names and regiments of any stragglers.

(c) On arrival at billets Battalions will at once clear all main roads. This order must be impressed on billeting parties so that they can make arrangements for it to be carried out.

(d) The front and rear section of fours of each Battalion will be detailed as an aeroplane guard.

(e) The order of march of Regimental 1st line transport will be as follows:-

> Pack animals in rear of their companies.
>
> <u>In rear of the Battalion.</u>
>
> M.G. limbers.
> Limbered wagons for M.G. ammunition.
> S.A.A. carts.
> Tool carts.
> Maltese carts.
> Water carts.
> Travelling kitchens.
> Cooks wagons.
> Spare animals.
> *Transport Sergt.*

(f) Water carts and water bottles will be full.

(g) Marching out states will reach Brigade H.Q. an hour before the head of the Brigade passes the starting point.

RELIEFS, etc.

Officers, N.C.Os and men from the 3rd Canadian Brigade to relieve the undermentioned will arrive at LOCRE Barrier at 3 p.m. tomorrow & guides will meet them there as stated below.

Locre Barrier	)
La Clytte Barrier	) Guide provided by 1st Suffolk Regt.
Kemmel Guards.	)
G.H.Q.Caretakers, N 20 a 5.3	)
-- do -- Arcadia.	) 1 man from each these places provided under orders of Bde:M.G.Officer.
-- do -- Vierstraat Line	)
Tramway Section	)
Brigade Pioneers.	)
Mining Section.	) Guide by Bde:Mining Officer. 1 officer & 36 men only, will arrive to replace 1 officer & 29 men of 6th Welch Regt & 9 men 2nd N.Fusiliers. Remainder of Mining Section remain until further orders.

Receipts to be taken for all tools, grenades, shelters, etc., handed over and forwarded by officer responsible for finding guides, to Brigade Headquarters.

ACCOMMODATION NIGHT OF 20th/21st.

Battalion.	Officers	Men.
1st Welch Regiment	Court-Martial House, Locre.	Locre, except school & row in line with Post Office, Farm M 25 d 5.8 & 22 large shelters.
6th Welch Regiment	Quartermasters present house.	Locre Schools, 23 bell tents pitched in field outside school.
2nd Northd:Fuslrs.	Court-Martial House, Locre.	Badajos huts, men in officers mess & officers huts, 12 bell tents & 74 small shelters-now pitched under orders of Q.M., 1st Welch Regt. 6 bell tents in transport lines.
2nd Cheshire Regt.	Locrehoff Farm	Locrehoff Farm & Locrehoff huts & 10 Bell tents.
1st Suffolk Regt.	Farm N 19 d 0.2	Farm N 19 d 0.2, Farm N 25 b 1.8 & 15 tents to be withdrawn by 1st Suffolk R. from Kemmel Shelters & pitched at Farm N 25 b 1.8

34 bell tents at Kemmel Shelters and 15 bell tents at Farm N 25 b 1.8 will be handed over to relieving Canadian Battalion at Kemmel Shelters. All other tents and shelters will be handed over to a Canadian billeting party on morning of 21st and receipts taken and forwarded to Brigade Headquarters.

It is regretted accommodation is very limited and units must make the best of what is provided.

S.P.A. Rolls

Captain,
Staff Captain,
84th Infantry Brigade.

19th Sept:1915.

Secret

OPERATION ORDER No.60,   Copy No. 4

by

Brigadier-General T.H.Finch-Pearse, C.M.G.,

Commanding 84th Infantry Brigade.

26th September 1915.

Reference Map
HAZEBROUCK 5a
1/100,000.

1. All troops in the 84th Brigade Area, less Divisional Ammunition Column, will march to MERVILLE today.

2. Route PETIT SEC BOIS - LARUE DU BOIS - VIEUX BERQUIN - NEUF BERQUIN to MERVILLE.

3. Starting point. Road junction just West of P in PETIT SEC BOIS.

84th Bde:Headqrs	8.15 a.m.	
6th Welch Regiment	8.18 a.m.	
1st Welch Regiment	8.24 a.m.	
2nd Northd:Fusiliers	8.31 a.m.	will not march through
1st Suffolk Regiment	8.38 a.m.	STRAZEELE.
2nd Cheshire Regt.	8.45 a.m.	
Remainder of 1st Line Transport of 84th Infantry Bde: under Lieut:L.C.Frisby, 6th Welch Regiment	8.52 a.m.	1.52
2nd Northumbrian Field Company, R.E.	.. a.m.	1.57
85th Field Ambulance	9.1 a.m.	
31st Brigade R.F.A.	9.5 a.m.	
130th Howitzer Bde,R.A.	9.25 a.m.	
No.3 Coy:A.S.C.	9.35 a.m.	

4. Remainder of 1st Line Transport of 84th Brigade will form up in order of march of units, head clear of X Roads just South of LL in PRADELLES by 8.27 a.m. Thence to starting point.

5. Billeting parties will meet Staff Captain at Road Junction due W of B in LA BRIANNE (⅔ mile N.E.of MERVILLE) at 7.15 a.m.

6. Headqrs, 28th Division, at Hotel DE VILLE MERVILLE after 7 a.m. to-day.

E C Gapp

Major,
Brigade Major,
84th Infantry Brigade.

Issued at 4 p.m.

No. 1 Retained.
No. 2 2nd Northd:Fuslrs.
No. 3 1st Suffolk Regt.
✓ No. 4 2nd Cheshire Regt.
No. 5 1st Welch Regiment.
No. 6 6th Welch Regiment.

No. 7 31st Brigade, R.F.A.
No. 8 130th Howitzer Bde:R.A.
No. 9 2/1st Northumbrian Field
No.10 No.3 Coy:A.S.C.(Coy:R.E.
No.11 85th Field Ambulance.
No.12 Staff Captain, 84th Bde.

Copy No. 4

84th Infantry Brigade Operation Order No.62.

September 29th 1915.

Secret

1. The 83rd and 85th Infantry Brigades take over trench line from G 12 a 5.4 to about G 4 a 4.5. 83rd Brigade on the right. Point of junction between Brigades will be INRUTOIRE-HAISNES Road, about G 5 c 6.9.
2. Relief will be completed by night 29th/30th September.
3. The 84th Infantry Brigade will remain in 1st Corps Reserve.

Issued at 10 a.m.

Major,
Brigade Major,
84th Infantry Brigade.

No.1 Retained.
No.2 2nd Northd: Fusiliers.
No.3 1st Suffolk Regiment.
No.4 2nd Cheshire Regiment.
No.5 1st Welch Regiment.
No.6 6th Welch Regiment.

No 4

84th Bde. Operation Order No. 67

5-10-11

1. Brigade moves tomorrow to billets in the area BERGUETTE - GAURBECQUE - BUSNES.

Brigade H.Q.
2nd N. Fus:
1st Suffolk R
1st Welch R
2nd Ches: R
1st Welch R
No 3 Coy A.S.C

2. Starting point - junction of RUE DE LILLE and RUE MARCELLIN BERTHELOT (fourth turning to the North going West from Bde H.Q.) thence by RUE VICTOR HUGO - CHOCQUES - BUSNES. Head of Brigade will pass the starting point at 8 a.m. Order of march as in the margin. No 3 Coy A.S.C. will join the column near its billet.

3. Baggage wagons will accompany 1st Line transport.

E C Gepp Major
Bde Major
84th Infty Bde

Issued at 11.10 p.m.

No. 1 Returned
  2 2nd N. Fus.
  3 1st Suffolk R
  4 2nd Ches: R

No. 5 1st Welch R
  6 6th Welch R
  7 No 3 Coy A.S.C
  8 85th Field ambulance

Officers Commanding units will
send an officer in the morning
to reconnoitre the starting point.
Arrangements will be made by
units so that their Batts & Transport
is not standing about in the streets
but marches so as to arrive at the
starting point at the right time.

J.E. C[?] Major
Bde Major
84th Infy Bde

84th Bde.
28th Div.

Embarked with Bde. for Salonika 24.10.15.

2nd CHESHIRES

OCTOBER

1 9 1 5

Army Form C. 2118.

3RD. ECHELON, M.E.F.
13 NOV. 1915
CENTRAL REGISTRY.
No. M.F.C/

WAR DIARY
or
INTELLIGENCE SUMMARY.
(Erase heading not required.)

Instructions regarding War Diaries and Intelligence Summaries are contained in F.S. Regs., Part II, and the Staff Manual respectively. Title pages will be prepared in manuscript.

Hour, Date, Place.	Summary of Events and Information.	Remarks and references to Appendices.
3.30 p.m. 29 Sept. ANNEQUIN	Battn. marched to ANNEQUIN and billeted.	
9 a.m. 30 Sept.	Battn. practised in throwing bombs and grenades.	
5.30 p.m.	Proceeded to trenches via Vermelles and took over from Royal Fusiliers No 1 and No 2 Companies in the West Face of the Hohenzollern Redoubt, No 3 and 4 Companies in Support.	
Trenches Hohenzollern Redoubt		
5.30 a.m. 1st October	Relief completed.	
7 a.m.	Heavy fire from trench mortars and aerial torpedoes. 2/Lieut. Rivington and Hartley No 1 Coy. killed, 2/Lieut Jones bombing officer wounded. Enemy fired a warning whizz-bang on the Northumberland Fusiliers S.W. of Redoubt, a company of which came up 2/Lt. McGregor commanding No 2 Coy. killed, Capt. Freeman Actg. Adjutant - was sent forward to command No 2 Coy.	
12 noon	No 1 Company - Captain Dryden - was relieved by No 4 Company - Captain Lloyd.	
6 p.m.		
8 p.m.	No 3 Company - Capt. Maxwell - was brought forward from support trench to take part in an attack with No 4 Company on the CHORD, a strong trench running NORTH to SOUTH across the HOHENZOLLERN REDOUBT. Attack partially successful 2/Lieut. CAMERON, No 4 Company was wounded.	

Army Form C. 2118.

WAR DIARY
or
INTELLIGENCE SUMMARY.
(Erase heading not required.)

Instructions regarding War Diaries and Intelligence Summaries are contained in F. S. Regs., Part II, and the Staff Manual respectively. Title pages will be prepared in manuscript.

Hour, Date, Place.	Summary of Events and Information.	Remarks and references to Appendices.
5 am 2nd October	The enemy bombarded the two Companies holding the WEST FACE of the HOHENZOLLERN REDOUBT with Bombs Trench Mortars and Aerial Torpedoes. Bombardment was continued throughout the day.	
12 Midnight "	No 1 Company supported the Suffolk Regiment in an attack on the NORTH WEST FACE of the REDOUBT. Attack failed. Captain Ogden (Durham L.I.) and 2/Lieut. RAIKES were wounded. 2nd Lieut COLE rejoined Battalion on having completed a course in the use of the LEWIS Gun. Two LEWIS Guns were brought with him into the REDOUBT. Enemy continued bombardment throughout the night.	
7.30 am 3rd October	Captain Freeman was sent to command a party of the Northumberland Fusiliers on the SOUTH WEST of the REDOUBT, the two officers of this party having been wounded. Enemy bombing incessantly.	
7.45 am " "	The enemy delivered an unexpected attack on our left with Bombs and Machine Guns and eventually turned it. The Batt: fought well but were driven back. Enemy reoccupied WEST FACE.	

Gulab Singh & Sons, Calcutta—No. 22 Army C.—5-8-14—1,07,000.

Army Form C. 2118.

WAR DIARY
or
INTELLIGENCE SUMMARY.
(Erase heading not required.)

Instructions regarding War Diaries and Intelligence Summaries are contained in F. S. Regs., Part II, and the Staff Manual respectively. Title pages will be prepared in manuscript.

Hour, Date, Place.	Summary of Events and Information.	Remarks and references to Appendices.
	WEST FACE of the HOHENZOLLERN REDOUBT.	
	Major Hill + Captain Lloyd were killed 2/Lieuts: Paton, Morris and Alderley wounded, 7/Lieuts Cole and Brien missing.	
	Casualties from 30th September to 3rd October both dates inclusive :-	
	Killed Wounded Missing Total	
	Officers 5 7 2 14	
	Other Ranks 43 153 166 362	
5 PM 3rd October	Battalion was withdrawn to VERMELLES and slept the night in LANCASTER DUG OUTS	
11 AM 4th October	Battalion moved forward and occupied Reserve Trenches in relief of Suffolk Regt	
6 AM 5th October	Battalion was relieved by the Middlesex Regt and withdrew to ANNEQUIN	
6 PM "	Marched to BETHUNE and billeted for the night.	
8 AM 6th October	Marched to BUSNES for a rest.	Actg. Major NH joined Bn.
7th October	Stayput in inspecting arms equipment etc which have Newmany joined Bn.	
8th October	Drill throughout the day, to restore smartness and discipline, lessened by the trials undergone during the recent operations. 2/Lt. Morton proceeded to WISQUES to undergo a course in LEWIS GUN.	

WAR DIARY
or
INTELLIGENCE SUMMARY.

(Erase heading not required.)

Army Form C. 2118.

Hour, Date, Place.	Summary of Events and Information.	Remarks and references to Appendices.
BUSNES		
9th October	Drill. Digging of trench for the training of bombers. Baths allotted to Battn. at GUARABECQUE. 2/Lt King-Smith Wilts Regt. proceeded to BETHUNE for instruction in bombing.	Programme of work attached
10th October	Drill. Digging of trench for the training of bombers. Range allotted to Battn. at HOLLANDERUE. 96 men exercised.	Programme of work attached -do-
11th October	Drill. Battn. exercised in bombing. Captain Tillard, Manchester Regt. joined Battn. from 1st Cheshire Regt. Posted to No 4 Coy.	
12th October	Battalion Route March. Firing on 30 yards Range at HOLLANDERUE. 24 men per Company. The following Officers joined the Battn. from ROUEN:– 2/Lts Greet and Andrews 9/ ? Lincolns. Halsey 10th Bn. Wardle 14th Bn. Boddington 14th Bn. Tiedeman 14th Bn. Hartje 3/ Bn.	Programme of work attached
13th October	Close Order Drill and instruction in bombing. Range at Hollanderie allotted to Bn. 96 men exercised. 2/Lt. Morton rejoined from a Lewis Gun course at Wisques.	
14th October	Close order drill and instruction in bombing. Range at Hollanderie. 96 men exercised. Baths allotted to No 3 Company at LILLERS.	Programme of work attached
15th October	Inspected by the Divisional Commander - Major Genl. BRIGGS. Musketry Exercises. Lieut Andrews and 2 men proceeded to ST VENANT for instruction in STOKES MORTAR, and returned at night.	

Army Form O. 2118.

WAR DIARY
or
INTELLIGENCE SUMMARY.
(Erase heading not required.)

Instructions regarding War Diaries and Intelligence Summaries are contained in F. S. Regs., Part II, and the Staff Manual respectively. Title pages will be prepared in manuscript.

Hour, Date, Place.	Summary of Events and Information.	Remarks and references to Appendices.
BUSNES 16th October	Guest Score Brown R.A.M.C (attached, awarded Military Cross by the Tucker & Lewis (A.S.M) Instruction in trenching. Close Order Drill and Rifle Exercises, Musketry and Practising The Assault.	Programme attached
17th October	Baths allotted to No 1 Coy + Machine Gunners at GUARBECQUE. Sunday. Divine Service. No Drill Parades	
9.30 am 18th October	Battalion marched about 5 miles to a new billeting area just North of BETHUNE via BUSNETTES and CHOCQUES, arriving about 1 P.M. Battalion Hd Qrs Etamines 5/10 K.S. South of HINGES.	Bde. O.O. No 68 and Batts. O.O. 4/17.10.15
HINGES		
9 am 19th October	Companies at disposal of OC Companies.	
2.30 P.M " "	Battalion marched to LE QUESNOY and billeted.	Bde. O.O No. 69
5. P.M " "	An exceptionally heavy bombardment of German positions in front of Cuinchy lasting 2 hours.	and
7 P.M " "	All Maps excepting HAZEBROUCK 5/10, 2 Ed limbered wagons handed into Brigade and the One Lewis Gun in possession handed into Brigade Head Qrs. All leave stopped.	Batts. O.O. of 19/10/15
LE QUESNOY 20th October	Companies at disposal of OC Companies. Battalion on duty, prepared to march off at 1 hour's notice. Nine Heavy Draught Horses handed over Eighteen light Draught received in their place. Captain N.R. Freeman awarded Military Cross.	N.R Freeman Captain Ch Adjutant

Army Form C. 2118.

WAR DIARY
or
INTELLIGENCE SUMMARY.

(Erase heading not required.)

Instructions regarding War Diaries and Intelligence Summaries are contained in F.S. Regs., Part II, and the Staff Manual respectively. Title pages will be prepared in manuscript.

Hour, Date, Place.	Summary of Events and Information.	Remarks and references to Appendices.
LE QUESNOY		
1 PM 21st October	Major MORTON appointed to a command in England. No. 4 Company and 1st line Transport proceeded to FOUQUEREUIL Station via BETHUNE. No. 4 Company for fatigue duty loading baggage and vehicles on trucks.	Operation Orders attached
3 PM " "	Battalion paraded less No. 4 Coy. - and proceeded to FOUQUEREUIL Station. Reached station at 5.30 pm and entrained.	
6.30 PM " "	Departed for MARSEILLES.	
On TRAIN		
22nd & 23rd October	Battalion passed through ST POL, AMIENS, VILLENEUVE, MONTEREAU, MACON, LYON and PIERRELATT. Tea and Coffee was provided by the French Railway Authorities at MONTEREAU, MACON and PIERRELATT.	
MARSEILLES		
6 am 24th October	Battalion reached MARSEILLES and detrained.	
" " "	No. 1 Company - Lieut: LAW - detailed to off load stores and vehicles.	
7 am " "	Battalion - less No. 1 Company - marched to the Docks, distance about 8 miles.	
9 am " "	Arrived at MARSEILLES Docks and embarked on the S.S. IVERNIA Cunard Liner.	
10 am " "	Arrived at Docks of No. 1 Company and 1st line Transport.	
10.15 am " "	No. 1 Company embarked and 10 vehicles only of 1st line Transport put on, on account of insufficient room.	
10.30 am " "	Lieut. McAllister - Transport Officer - 31 other Ranks and 40 Horses Number embarked on S.S. IVERNIA - Officers 20, other Ranks 518.	

WAR DIARY
or
INTELLIGENCE SUMMARY

Army Form C. 2118.

(Erase heading not required.)

Instructions regarding War Diaries and Intelligence Summaries are contained in F. S. Regs., Part II, and the Staff Manual respectively. Title pages will be prepared in manuscript.

Hour, Date, Place.	Summary of Events and Information.	Remarks and references to Appendices.
No Heres		
11 am 24th October 15	Entrained on S.S. SHROPSHIRE. Twenty Six Transport men and 37 Horses with whicks that could not be loaded on the S.S. IVERNIA, were sent to a camp on the outskirts of MARSEILLES.	
S.S. IVERNIA		
4 P.M. 24th October 15	Weighed anchor and steamed in an easterly direction	
25th October 1915	Paraded for Rounds at 10.30 am and performed Physical Exercises 11am to 12 noon and 3 PM to 4 PM.	
" " "	Boats allotted to Companies, and men told off to their boats.	
5 PM " "	The "Warn" practised.	Regtl Orders attached
6 PM " "	Battalion on duty till 6 PM 26th October 1915.	
26th October 1915	Battalion paraded for Rounds at 10.30 am Physical Exercises 11am to 12 noon and 4 PM to 5 PM.	
27th October 1915	Battalion paraded for Rounds at 10.30 am Physical Exercises 11am to 12 noon and 4 PM to 5 PM. A rough day, many men sick.	
28th October 1915	Battalion paraded for Rounds at 10.30 am Physical Exercises 11am to 12 noon and 4 PM to 5 PM. Battalion on duty for 24 hours from 6 PM	
29th October 1915	Arrived at Alexandria and anchored (ALEXANDRIA)	Regtl Orders 27/10/15 attached
4.30 PM " " "	Weighed anchor and berthed in No 42 Quay	
7 PM " " "	No 3 Coy – CAPTAIN MAXWELL – on fatigue unloading	

N.B. Presumer to of line
at Regtl orderly Rm.

Army Form C. 2118

WAR DIARY
or
INTELLIGENCE SUMMARY.
(Erase heading not required.)

Instructions regarding War Diaries and Intelligence Summaries are contained in F. S. Regs., Part II, and the Staff Manual respectively. Title pages will be prepared in manuscript.

Hour, Date, Place.	Summary of Events and Information.	Remarks and references to Appendices.
6 AM 30th October 1915	Unloading Vehicles. No 4 Company — 2/Lt. TIEDEMAN — on fatigue unloading stores.	
6.30 AM " " "	Horses brought round from H.M.T. SHROPSHIRE.	Bde. Order
7 AM " " "	Transport moved by road to MARMOURA CAMP. distance about 12 miles.	and Train Time Table attached
9 AM " " "	No 1 and 2 Companies and Signallers entrained.	
9.15 AM " " "	Train departed with above for MARMOURA CAMP, arrived at 10.25 AM	
11.30 AM " " "	No 3 and 4 Companies and Machine Gunners entrained.	
11.40 AM " " "	Train departed with above for MARMOURA CAMP, arrived at 12.45 PM	
1 PM " " "	Transport arrived at MARMOURA CAMP.	
MARMOURA CAMP		
6.30 AM 31st October 1915	Battalion performed a short ROUTE MARCH.	
9.30 AM " " "	Battalion paraded for Divine Service.	
10.30 AM " " "	Companies at the disposal of Company Commanders.	
5 PM " " "	Battalion Bathing Parade.	

M.R Freeman Captain Rgt
Adjt of Cheshire Rgt

W Conolry Major
Comdg 2/1 Bn The Cheshire Rgt

www.ingramcontent.com/pod-product-compliance
Lightning Source LLC
Chambersburg PA
CBHW081536160426
43191CB00011B/1769